ALAN OCTOBER 2013

BRANCH LINES AROUND

BARRY

To Cardiff, Wenvoe, Penarth and Bridgend

Vic Mitchell and Keith Smith

MP Middleton Press

Cover picture: One of P & A Campbell's steamers is alongside Barry Pier in July 1953, as ex-Taff Vale Railway A class 0-6-2T no. 394 runs round its train. The long shadows indicate that it is evening time and so the passengers are in the train ready to return home. The roof of the walkway to the floating pontoon is almost horizontal, suggesting high tide; the far end could drop 40ft at low tide. (SLS coll.)

This book marks the achievement of the many individuals and authorities who made it possible to restore passenger services to 20 miles of Welsh railway in 2005.

Published March 2005

ISBN 1 904474 50 0

© *Middleton Press, 2005*

Design Deborah Esher

Published by
> *Middleton Press*
> *Easebourne Lane*
> *Midhurst, West Sussex*
> *GU29 9AZ*

Tel: 01730 813169
Fax: 01730 812601
Email: info@middletonpress.co.uk
www.middletonpress.co.uk

Printed & bound by Biddles Ltd, Kings Lynn

CONTENTS

INDEX

ACKNOWLEDGEMENTS

We are very grateful for the assistance received from many of those mentioned in the credits also to J.F.Andrews, L.Crosier, G.Croughton, T.Hancock, F.Hornby, J.B.Horne, N.Langridge, M.Messenger, D.T.Rowe, Mr D. and Dr S.Salter, L.Turner, M.Turvey and particularly our ever supportive wives, Barbara Mitchell and Janet Smith.

1. The 1947 Railway Clearing House map omits the line between Cowbridge and Aberthaw, as it had closed earlier.

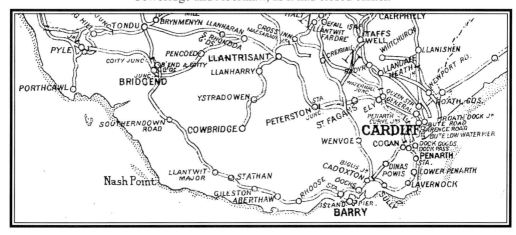

GEOGRAPHICAL SETTING

We will consider the district from east to west and generalise by stating that the Cardiff-Barry area is composed of fairly level Marls. However, the line passes through a narrow ridge of Limestone at Cogan, this outcrop also being evident north and south of the seaside residential town of Penarth, running as far south as Lavernock. The substantial Ely River is a notable feature north of Cogan; Penarth Dock was formed on its south bank.

The minor watercourse of the Sully Brook and the Cadoxton River converge to the east of Barry Dock, which was built in an area northeast of Barry Island, another Limestone outcrop.

The remaining lines covered by this album were almostly entirely built on Limestone, the route northwards requiring a tunnel more than one mile in length north of Wenvoe for the Barry Railway's main line to penetrate the ridge. West of Barry, the railway required two tunnels and a viaduct to reach the undulating plateau of the Vale of Glamorgan. The River Thaw once provided suitable conditions for a small port at its estuary at Aberthaw. The other waterway of note is the Ewenny River, crossed on the approach to the old established commercial centre of Bridgend.

The routes were in the county of Glamorgan until 1974 and then South Glamorgan until 1996. Since that time, the eastern end has been in a unitary authority covering the Cardiff area. Penarth westwards (excepting Bridgend) came under one known as the Vale of Glamorgan Council.

The maps are to the scale of 25ins to 1 mile with north at the top, unless otherwise indicated.

HISTORICAL BACKGROUND

Late upon the scene, the Barry Railway was rooted deep in the history of South Wales railways. The Taff Vale Railway was one of the main coal carriers to the docks at Cardiff and in 1840 it began a passenger service from Abercynon to Bute Dock, the track being standard gauge.

The first main line in the area was that of the South Wales Railway, which opened between Chepstow and Swansea in 1850 and became part of the Great Western Railway in 1862. It was broad gauge (7ft 0¼ins) until 1872.

The frustration of the Bute Dock monopoly resulted in the TVR's colliery customers obtaining an Act of Parliament on 21st July 1856 for the Ely Tidal Harbour & Railway. The latter diverged from the 1840 route at Radyr, its six-mile length forming a north-south bypass to Cardiff. It opened on 4th July 1859 and the southern part was operated by the Penarth Harbour Dock & Railway Company initially.

A further Act of 27th July 1857 was for the Penarth Harbour, Dock & Railway on the opposite side of the Ely River. The two-mile line, together with the route from Radyr, was leased to the TVR from 1864. The dock opened on 10th June 1865, the railway pre-dating it for the conveyance of construction materials.

The line from Cardiff to Penarth conveyed passengers from 20th February 1878, when the route was extended to a station near the town centre. It reached Lavernock on 1st December 1887, Sully on 24th December 1888, Biglis Junction (near Cadoxton) on 8th July 1889 and finally Cadoxton on 22nd May 1890.

The TVR, the Rhymney Railway and the owners of Cardiff Docks controlled the cost of conveyance of all exported coal and so a group of colliery owners obtained an Act on 14th August 1885 for the Barry Dock & Railways Company, which would give them independence. The route would cross, and have links into, several coal producing valleys and have a short main line, well to the west of Cardiff. The southern part opened for freight on 13th May 1889, a branch to Cogan having opened to passengers from Barry Dock on 20th December 1888. The docks were first filled with water on 29th June and the main line completed for the opening ceremony on 18th July 1889. The Barry Dock to Barry section carried passengers from 8th February 1889 and goods from 13th May following.

The railway from Barry to Bridgend (and Coity Junction) via Llantwit Major, was authorised by the Vale of Glamorgan Railway Act of 26th August 1889 and opened on 1st December 1897. It was worked by the Barry Railway and was designed to bring coal to the docks from valleys in the Bridgend area. It crossed the 1892 TVR line from Cowbridge west of Aberthaw.

The BD&R Co. name was changed to the Barry Railway in 1891, but it was always known as the "Barry". The enterprise was an immense success, not only in the area of coal conveyance, but a massive passenger business developed conveying workers in both directions simultaneously between Barry and Cardiff.

The line was extended to Barry Island on 3rd

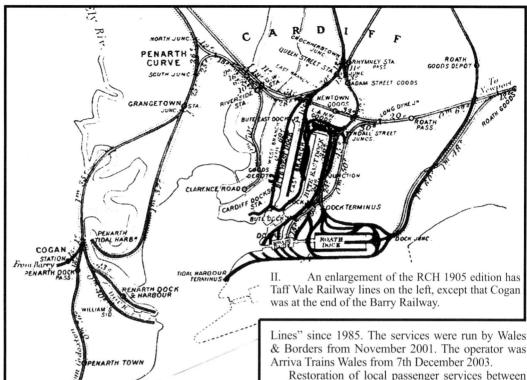

II. An enlargement of the RCH 1905 edition has Taff Vale Railway lines on the left, except that Cogan was at the end of the Barry Railway.

August 1896, the route through Wenvoe having a regular passenger service from 16th March of that year. This became the Barry's main line. Thus leisure traffic from the valleys and the Cardiff district became a third area for profit. A further extension to Barry Pier on 27th June 1899 led to yet a fourth one - steamer operation across the Bristol Channel, notably to Weston-super-Mare. However, restrictions limited its success; it did not start until 1904 and ceased in 1910, but other operators prospered.

The 1921 Railways Act resulted in the Barry becoming a constituent of the GWR on 1st January 1922. Few railways of only 68 route miles had been such a success; 2.75m passengers (*excluding* season ticket holders) had been carried in its final year.

Nationalisation on 1st January 1948 brought the docks and railways under separate control, the latter coming into the Western Region of British Railways. Passenger services were withdrawn from the Wenvoe route on 10th September 1962 and from the Vale of Glamorgan line on 15th June 1964. The latter was retained for freight and as a diversionary route. The Wenvoe line closed completely on 2nd December 1963 and the Cadoxton-Penarth route followed likewise on 6th May 1968.

Following privatisation, trains were operated by the Cardiff Railway Co. Ltd (Prism Rail plc) from 13th October 1996. Trains had been branded "Valley Lines" since 1985. The services were run by Wales & Borders from November 2001. The operator was Arriva Trains Wales from 7th December 2003.

Restoration of local passenger services between Barry and Bridgend, albeit with only two intermediate stations initially, was proposed for June 2005.

Preservation Era

The survival of about 200 of Britain's 16,000 steam locomotives was a result of a batch remaining intact in Woodham's Scrapyard, which had been established on sidings in part of Barry Docks in 1959. Loco cutting mainly ceased in 1965 and sales for preservation began in 1968, this continuing until 1986. Several books have been written on the topic and so our comments are limited.

More recent preservation has been centred on Barry Island, where the 1994 Vale of Glamorgan Railway began a short passenger operation on 2nd May 1998. The company had evolved from the 1977 Butetown Historic Railway Society, which had operated at Bute Road station in Cardiff, the former TVR HQ. The Cardiff Bay development scheme did not include industrial heritage and so most of the enforced move took place in 1997. This included ten ex-Barry Scrapyard hulks - "The Barry Ten".

The early service was restricted to Barry Island itself, but running to the mainland began on 12th April 2001. Details of the stations thereon are given under photos 13 to 18, which feature the VoGR. It was rebranded as the Barry Steam Railway in 2004.

There are an exceptionally high number of discrepancies in the records of dates relating to the Barry area and we consider the ones quoted are the most likely.

III. A 4ins to 1 mile map of 1869 shows the freight-only Penarth Railway, officially the Penarth Harbour, Dock & Railway, and leased to the Taff Vale Railway, with dashes to indicate the proposed routes.

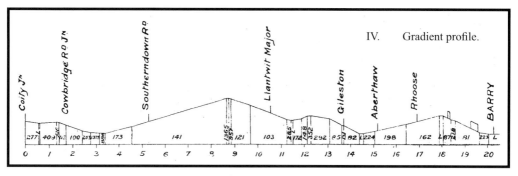

IV.   Gradient profile.

V.   The full extent of the Barry Railway and its connections to other companies totalled 68 route miles. Only the southern part is contained in this album.

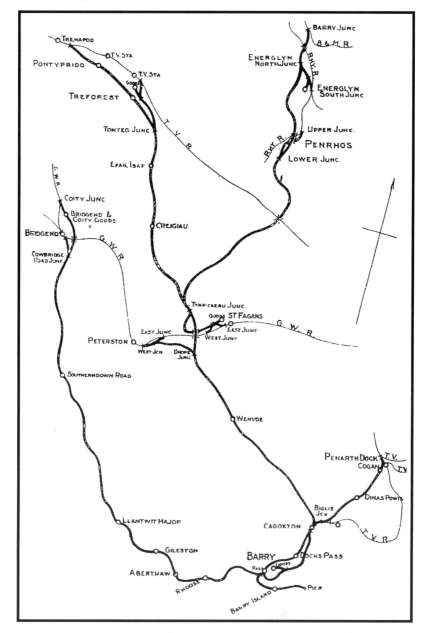

PASSENGER SERVICES

Cardiff and Penarth

The TVR's initial service was one of eight trains between Cardiff and Penarth, weekdays only, calling at Penarth Dock. The figure had increased to 15 by January 1888, and two were extended to Lavernock. There were two to Penarth on Sundays. By May 1889 there were 17 on weekdays, four of which ran on to Sully.

Sully was still only receiving four trains in 1899, but they all continued to Cadoxton from 1890. There were three on Sundays.

The Barry's first timetable showed seven weekday and four Sunday trains between Cogan and Barry only. They ran to and from Cardiff Riverside (part of General after 1940) from 14th August 1893, with 18 on weekdays and 7 on Sundays. The frequency increased steadily and will not be detailed further, neither will the timetable north of Penarth. South thereof, a modest frequency continued and, by 1939, Sully was receiving 25 weekday and 12 Sunday trains. The numbers continuing to Cadoxton were 15 and 11.

From 1953, there was a marked increase in the service via Sully from Cardiff to Barry and in 1966, there were ten trains via Sully to Cadoxton or beyond, with three on Sundays. From 5th March 1967, the figure was eight daily, with one terminating at Sully, but they shuttled between Penarth and Cadoxton only.

Via Wenvoe

The service between Pontypridd and Barry remained at three on weekdays and two on Sundays throughout its 66 years, with minor adjustments. Examples are the addition of an 8.12am from Wenvoe to Barry in the early 1920s and closure of Wenvoe on Sundays from the 1930s. The conveyance of workers between the valleys and the docks was on a small scale, but leisure traffic to Barry Island brought some extra scheduled trains (particularly on Sundays and Thursdays) plus many excursions from selected locations, often at the heads of the valleys.

To Barry Island

The Summer timetables for 1897, 1898 and 1921 showed 8, 10 and 21 weekday trains, with 3 or 4 on Sundays. By the 1930s, there were two or three *per hour* at peak holiday times. Trains ran to the Pier only to make connection with boats. Most trains have continued to Barry Island since dieselisation in 1958.

Expresses

The "Ilfracombe Boat Express" ran non-stop between Cardiff and Barry Pier for a few Summers around 1906. The "Ports-to-Ports Express" was operated jointly by a number of companies from 1906 until 1914 between Barry and Newcastle, largely for the benefit of mariners. Between the wars, it was extended to Swansea and was a rare example of a scheduled express along the coast of Glamorgan. It ran via Penarth briefly, around 1922.

Vale of Glamorgan

The development of a large RAF base near St. Athan during World War II altered the traffic pattern, increasing it at the east end. The table shows the number of trains per day each side of Llantwit Major in selected years.

	West		East	
	Weekdays	Sundays	Weekdays	Sundays
1898	6	3	6	3
1921	8	0	11	3
1944	7	0	15	5
1964	3	0	10	0

Revival

The basic service since 1987 has been three trains to Penarth and three to Barry per hour. It was proposed that there would be one an hour to Bridgend from the line's reopening. The basic Penarth and Barry figures were expected to increase to four in December 2005.

CARDIFF, COGAN, and BARRY.—Barry.   [**Sundays.**

(Sample timetable — columns headed mrn/aft for down and up services)

Down:
Queen St. Sta., Cardiff (TV) dp.; Cogan; Dinas Powis; Cadoxton; Barry Dock; Barry arr.

Up:
Barry dep.; Barry Dock; Cadoxton; Dinas Powis; Cogan; Cardiff * 55.

b Arrives on Saturdays only.   * Queen Street Station.

MERTHYR, ABERDARE, COWBRIDGE, CARDIFF, PENARTH, and SULLY.—Taff Vale.

Down.		Week Days.		Sndys

High Street,
Merthyr (G.W.) d
Pentrebach *
Troedyrhiw
Merthyr Vale. [33
Quaker's Yard J

Aberdare d
Treaman
Mountain A
Penrhiwcebr
Aberdare J.

Aberdare Jn. 32

Treherbert
Treorky
Ystrad
Llwynpia
Dinas

Ferndale d
Tylors Twn
Ynishir
Porth arr

Porth
Havod
Pontypridd J

Pontypridd Junc.
Treforest

Church Village
Llantwit
Cross Inn
Llantris-{ arr
sant 34 { dep
Llanharry
Ystradowen
Cowbridge arr

Walnut Tree Bdg
Radyr
Llandaff
Cardiff

Cardiff ...dep
Cardiff Docks a

Cardiff (T.V.) dep
Cardiff (G.W.) 35
Grange Town
Penarth Dock 37
Penarth { arr { dep

Lavernock
Sully arr

May 1889   June 1897

Down.

Cardiff { Clarence R. d
(G.W.) { Riverside †
Grangetown
Cogan *
Dinas Powis

Porth dep.
Hafod
Pontyp. 'd (B.R.)
Efail Isa
Creigian
Wenvoe

Oadoxton (see above)
Barry Dock
Barry
Barry Island arr.

SUNDAYS.

* Adjoins Penarth Dock Station.   † Adjoins Main Line Station.   b Except Saturdays to and from Clarence Road.

June 1961

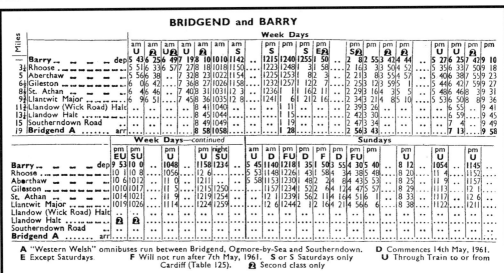

BRIDGEND and BARRY

Week Days

Miles		am	am	am	am	am	am	pm		pm	pm	pm		pm		pm	pm	pm	pm

— Barry ... dep
3¼ Rhoose
5 Aberthaw
6¼ Gileston
8½ St. Athan
9¾ Llantwit Major
11¼ Llandow (Wick Road) Halt
13¼ Llandow Halt
15 Southerndown Road
19 Bridgend A arr

Week Days—continued   **Sundays**

Barry ... dep
Rhoose
Aberthaw
Gileston
St. Athan
Llantwit Major
Llandow (Wick Road) Halt
Llandow Halt
Southerndown Road
Bridgend A arr

A "Western Welsh" omnibuses run between Bridgend, Ogmore-by-Sea and Southerndown.   D Commences 14th May, 1961.
E Except Saturdays.   F Will not run after 7th May, 1961.   S or S Saturdays only   U Through Train to or from Cardiff (Table 125).   2 Second class only

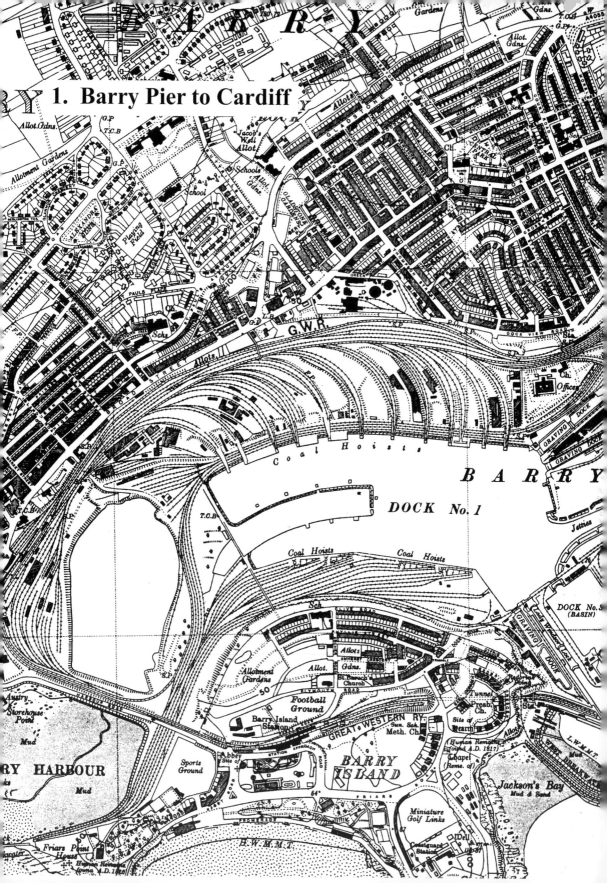

1. Barry Pier to Cardiff

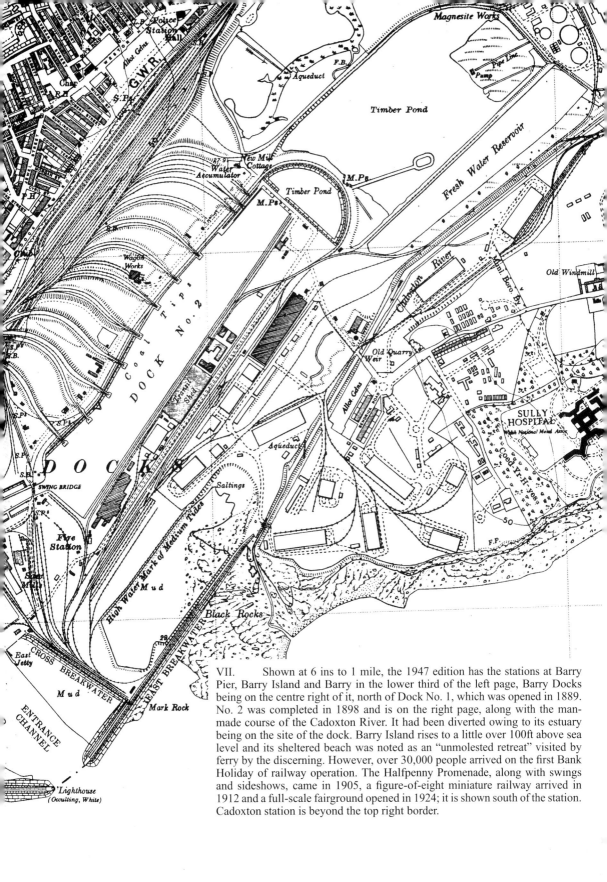

VII.　　　Shown at 6 ins to 1 mile, the 1947 edition has the stations at Barry Pier, Barry Island and Barry in the lower third of the left page, Barry Docks being on the centre right of it, north of Dock No. 1, which was opened in 1889. No. 2 was completed in 1898 and is on the right page, along with the man-made course of the Cadoxton River. It had been diverted owing to its estuary being on the site of the dock. Barry Island rises to a little over 100ft above sea level and its sheltered beach was noted as an "unmolested retreat" visited by ferry by the discerning. However, over 30,000 people arrived on the first Bank Holiday of railway operation. The Halfpenny Promenade, along with swings and sideshows, came in 1905, a figure-of-eight miniature railway arrived in 1912 and a full-scale fairground opened in 1924; it is shown south of the station. Cadoxton station is beyond the top right border.

BARRY PIER

VIII.　　The 1936 map shows the track layout which was in use until 5th May 1929, the tunnel on the left having double track to Barry Island until that time. The second tunnel connected the West Breakwater tracks with those of the docks. All tracks south of No. 1 Dock have been lifted, save those set into the quayside at a tank farm, but the West Breakwater high level track was still in place in 2005 (bottom centre). The hydraulic lift shown was never used after World War II.

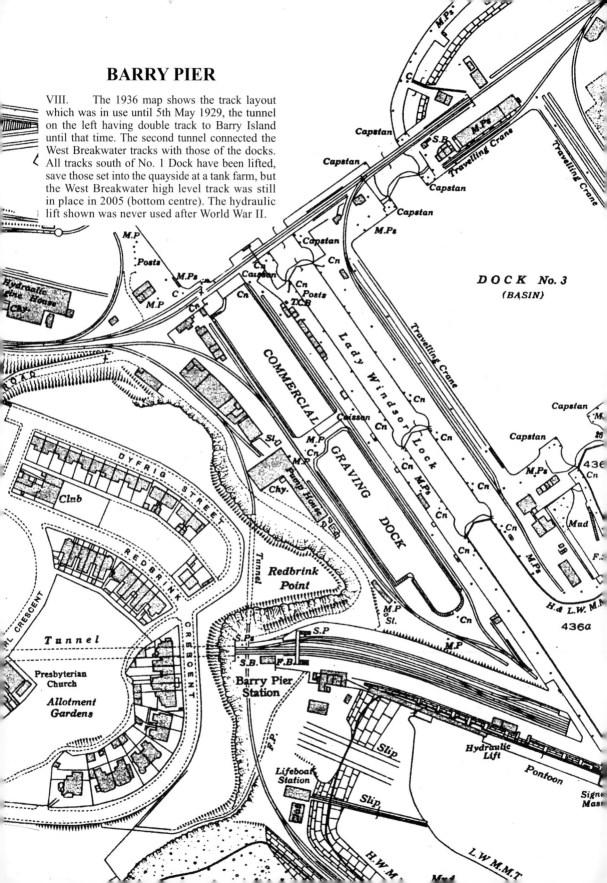

1.   A postcard view from above the tunnel mouth has West Breakwater on the right and the steamer pontoon adjacent to the up platform. The roofless part of the station in this view from about 1912 was for the use of gentlemen. An hydraulic passenger lift was also provided to convey passengers from the far end of the platform to and from the floating pontoon. (Lens of Sutton coll.)

2.   A Barry class E tank is leaving West Breakwater on removable rails, which were laid over the running lines when necessary. The arm with an S allowed locomotives to shunt into the tunnel. The signal box is included in the next picture. The crossing was last used in about 1968. (B.J.Miller coll.)

3.	The points for the loop remained in the tunnel following its track singling. The signal box (centre) was functional until September 1952. The removal of the other platform line took place sometime after 1953; the photo is from about 1956. Steamer passengers used the gate on the left during most non-wartime Summers from 27th June 1899 until 18th October 1971. There was a visit by a railtour in 1973 and the track was lifted in 1976. Another view can be found on the cover of this book. The area was later partly used by the Barry Yacht Club and the tunnel became a rifle range. (M.J.Stretton coll.)

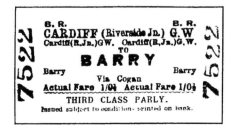

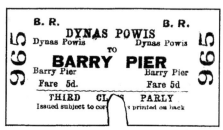

BARRY ISLAND

4.   This view towards the tunnel is from prior to 1908 when a siding was added at the far end of the up platform. This line served an excursion platform from 1914. The signal box in the distance was the only one until 5th May 1929, when the platform on the left became an island. There was a staff of seven at that time. (Lens of Sutton coll.)

5.   The shelter on the right was used by those waiting to join a train at the excursion platform (No. 2). The line to the right of 0-6-2T no. 389 in July 1950 is to Barry Pier. East Box was in use from 1929 until 10th May 1964, when the crossover was removed. It had 54 levers. (P.J.Garland/ R.S.Carpenter)

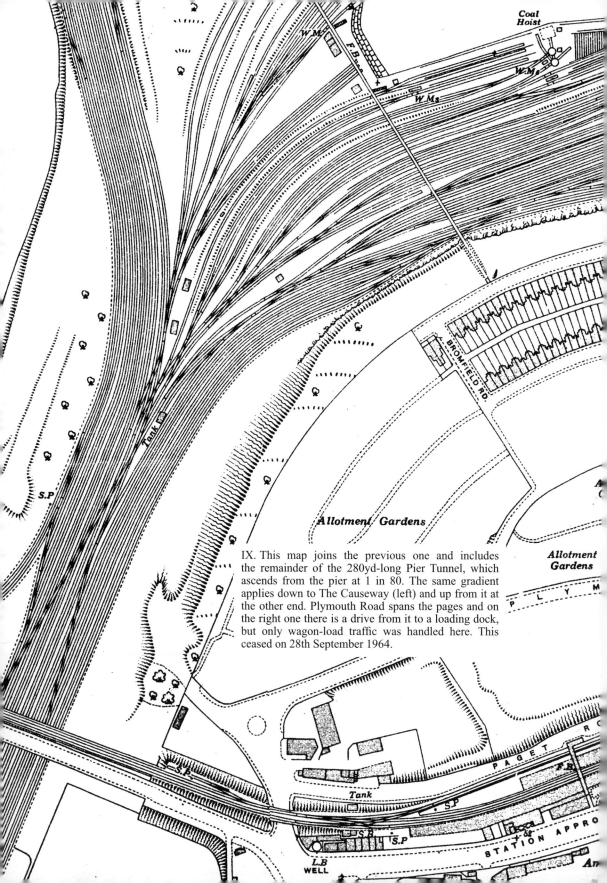

Coal Hoist

W.M⁸

F.B.

W.M⁸

W.Ms

Tank No⁴

BROMFIELD RD.

S.P.

Allotment Gardens

Allotment Gardens

P L Y M

IX. This map joins the previous one and includes the remainder of the 280yd-long Pier Tunnel, which ascends from the pier at 1 in 80. The same gradient applies down to The Causeway (left) and up from it at the other end. Plymouth Road spans the pages and on the right one there is a drive from it to a loading dock, but only wagon-load traffic was handled here. This ceased on 28th September 1964.

S.P.

Tank

S.P.

PAGET R

F.B.

STATION APPRO

52

L.B. WELL

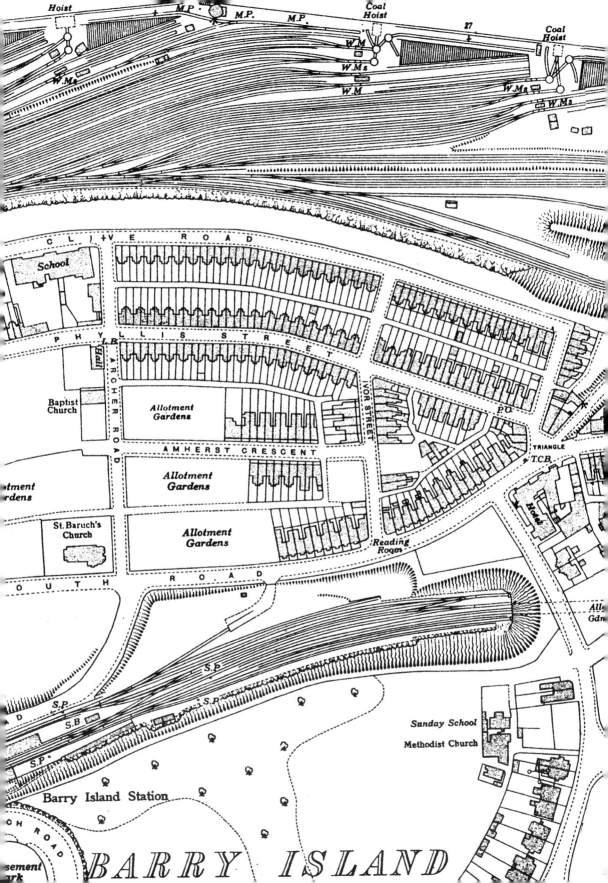

Hoist

M.P.   M.P.   M.P.

Coal Hoist

27

Coal Hoist

W.M
W.Ms
W.M

W.Ms

W.Ms

W.Ms

C L I V E   R O A D

School

P H Y L L I S   S T R E E T

Baptist Church

A R C H E R   R O A D

L.B.   Hall

Allotment Gardens

N O R   S T R E E T

P.O.

TRIANGLE

T.C.B.

Hotel

A M H E R S T   C R E S C E N T

Allotment Gardens

Allotment Gardens

otment dens

St. Baruch's Church

Allotment Gardens

Reading Room

All Gdn

S O U T H   R O A D

S.P.

S.P.

S.B.

S.P.

S.P.

Sanday School
Methodist Church

Barry Island Station

H   R O A D

sement rk

B A R R Y   I S L A N D

6.	Ex-LNWR class G2 0-8-0 no. 49409 has just used the crossover, having arrived with an excursion from Brynmawr on 14th July 1957. The crowds emerge for a day at the attractions, while the locomotive would turn on West Pond triangle in Barry Docks and then rest. (T.J.Edginton)

7.	A 1959 record of the south elevation includes loudspeakers for crowd control and stone carvings in the gable ends bearing "B.R" and "1896". The canopy was scrapped and the snack bar under the white gable became derelict, but the former was restored in 1995 and the latter became the main entrance to the VoGR shop and ticket office. (R.M.Casserley)

8.   Platforms 1, 3 and 4 are included in this view from the early 1960s; DMUs had been introduced on local services in 1958. The footbridge later lost its roof, but the platform canopy was extensively renovated in 1995, although not for use by Cardiff passengers. (Lens of Sutton coll.)

9.   West Box had 39 levers and functioned from 1929 until 15th March 1998. It was photographed in May 1964, along with part of The Causeway and the 153yd long Barry Island Viaduct. This part of the route was singled on 9th June 1969. (B.P.Mills)

10.   From left to right is Plymouth Road, the loading dock, four berthing sidings (behind them is a shelter for diesel fuelling), the sunken line to Barry Pier and the excursion platform with its associated toilet block. This was still standing in 2005, although the platform was closed in July 1976, when the number of tracks was reduced to two. This view is from the signal box in 1963. (B.P.Mills)

11.   Cardiff trains used only the western end of platform 1 after the signal box closure, as witnessed on 16th August 2001 as "Pacer" no. 143623 waits to depart. Behind the train, the track was later boarded over to give level access beween platforms 1 and 3/4. (M.J.Stretton)

BARRY - Preservation Era

12.   Initially Woodham's Scrapyard cut up mainly ex-GWR locos, but many later engines followed. This is the scene in October 1982 with RESERVED painted on the decaying cladding of one survivor. In the background is the chimney of one of the three hydraulic pumping stations which supplied water at 800 psi to operate hoists, cranes, dock gates and so on. One pump was electrified in 1925 and the other eight followed in 1935. (T.Heavyside)

13.   This telephoto view on 30th May 2001 is from the Barry Island station footbridge and in the same direction as picture no. 10. The VoGR was fortunate financially in having support from the Welsh Development Agency and other bodies, this allowing the construction of a GWR-style goods shed to serve as a workshop, exhibition hall and station, known as Plymouth Road. Their operational DMU and static 2-6-2T, no. 5538, are evident. (P.G.Barnes)

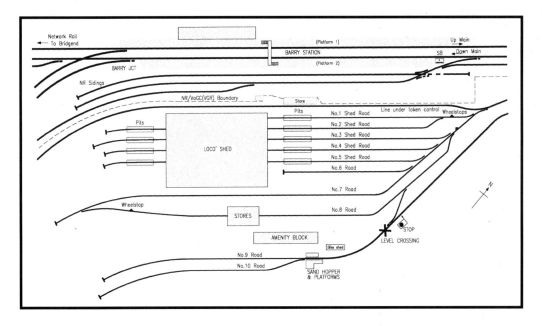

Network Rail
← To Bridgend

(Platform 1)

Up Main

BARRY STATION

Down Main

SB

BARRY JCT

NR Sidings

(Platform 2)

NR/VoGC(VGR) Boundary

Store

Line under token control

Wheelstops

Pits

No.1 Shed Road

Pits

No.2 Shed Road

No.3 Shed Road

LOCO' SHED

No.4 Shed Road

No.5 Shed Road

No.6 Road

No.7 Road

N

Wheelstop

STORES

No.8 Road

STOP

LEVEL CROSSING

AMENITY BLOCK

Bike shed

No.9 Road

No.10 Road

SAND HOPPER
& PLATFORMS

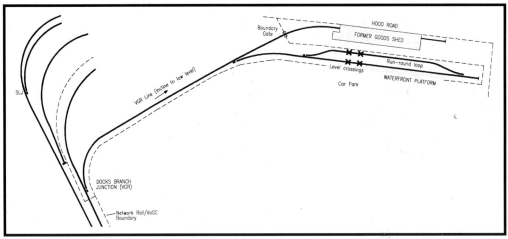

HOOD ROAD

Boundary
Gate

FORMER GOODS SHED

Run-round loop

Level crossings

WATERFRONT PLATFORM

SLJ

VGR Line (Incline to low level)

Car Park

DOCKS BRANCH
JUNCTION (VGR)

Network Rail/VoGC
Boundary

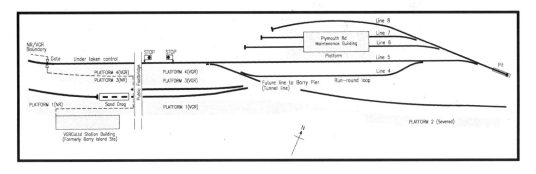

Line 8

Line 7

NR/VGR
Boundary

Plymouth Rd
Maintenance Building

Line 6

Gate

Under token control

STOP

STOP

Platform

Line 5

Pit

PLATFORM 4(VGR)

PLATFORM 4(VGR)

PLATFORM 3(NR)

PLATFORM 3(VGR)

Future line to Barry Pier
(Tunnel line)

Line 4

Run-round loop

PLATFORM 1(NR)

Sand Drag

PLATFORM 1(VGR)

Public Footbridge

VGRCoLtd Station Building
(Formerly Barry Island Stn)

N

PLATFORM 2 (Severed)

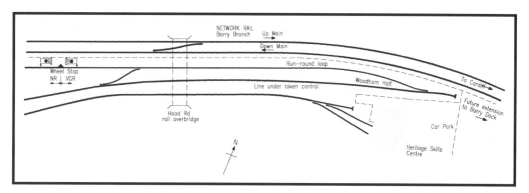

X.   VoGR track diagram in 2004, when the name was changed to the Barry Steam Railway for marketing purposes. The journey from Plymouth Road to Woodham Halt runs from lower left to upper right, but with some gaps. (B.P.Mills)

14.   The 1996 building is seen from above the tunnel mouth in March 2002, with Peckett 0-6-0ST *Sir Gomer* attached to the DMU trailer. This locomotive could not be used on the viaduct as its coupling rods would foul the raised guard rails outside the track thereon. (J.Morgan)

15. We move towards Barry Island Viaduct on 2nd July 2000 as new timber waybeams had recently been fitted in readiness for VoGR services to commence to the mainland on 12th April 2001. The guard rails on the operational line are evident; the 15mph speed limit was soon reduced to 10 and applied to both tracks. (B.P.Mills)

16. For 2001-03, the VoGR established a temporary northern terminus at Hood Road, adjacent to the former goods shed, shown at the bottom of map XII (after picture 30). Hunslet 0-6-0ST *Pamela* is returning to Barry Island in June 2001, its smoke drifting over the offices once used by Barry Railway goods clerks, but by then serving to house some of the staff of the *PS Waverley* and the *MV Balmoral*. (J.Morgan)

17.   *Pamela* is at the present Hood Road platform in August 2003 and alongside is ex-GWR 0-6-0PT no. 7754, a visitor from the Llangollen Railway. A Barry Railway coach was being restored in the goods shed, access being north of the offices. (J.Morgan)

18.   A further terminus was available from 8th April 2004, it being situated north of the original one and adjacent to the Skills Centre. Having just run round its train at Woodhams Halt in August 2004 is *Jessie*, a 1937 0-6-0ST from Hunslet on loan from the Llangollen Railway. (J.Morgan)

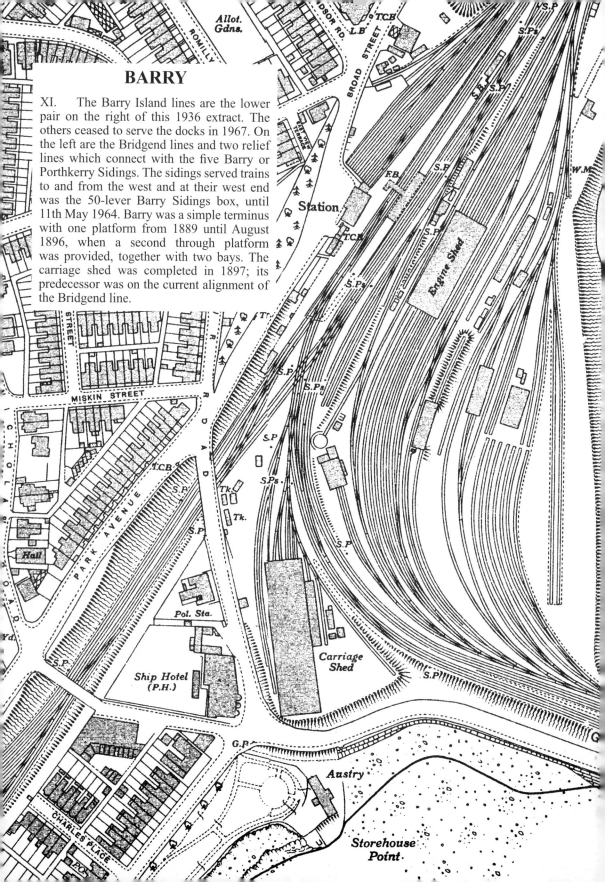

BARRY

XI.   The Barry Island lines are the lower pair on the right of this 1936 extract. The others ceased to serve the docks in 1967. On the left are the Bridgend lines and two relief lines which connect with the five Barry or Porthkerry Sidings. The sidings served trains to and from the west and at their west end was the 50-lever Barry Sidings box, until 11th May 1964. Barry was a simple terminus with one platform from 1889 until August 1896, when a second through platform was provided, together with two bays. The carriage shed was completed in 1897; its predecessor was on the current alignment of the Bridgend line.

19.   A train from Barry Island enters the up platform behind one of the BR's six new 2-4-2Ts, classified J. Numbered 86-91, the first three were built by Hudswell Clarke in 1897 and the others were from Sharp Stewart in 1898. There was a passenger staff of 120 recorded here in 1929. Note that there is an up signal amongst telegraph poles in the background. It is remote from the track to enhance visibility. (R.M.Casserley coll.)

20.   The BR's double-banded somersault centre-pivoted signal arms are seen more clearly in this view, which features class B1 0-6-2T no. 60 with a train for Bridgend. Note also the complex goods signals on the right, used before the introduction of route indicators. The great width of the up platform was probably due to track realignment in 1896; the canopy was added in 1900. (B.J.Miller coll.)

21.   The BR converted three 2-4-0Ts to 2-4-2Ts; this is no. 22 and it is in the carriage sidings north of the up platform on 24th July 1922. This was the site of the first goods yard. The engine was one of only four in the Barry fleet to have steam heating connections. (R.S.Carpenter coll.)

22.　Compartment stock leads in this train from Cardiff headed by ex-TVR A class 0-6-2T no. 373 in July 1950. The footbridge lost its roof a few years later and the bridge itself was replaced in April 1993. (P.J.Garland/R.S.Carpenter)

23.　A panorama from July 1959 includes the 8.10am for Bridgend on the left and a fitter under the 7.45 for Pontypridd via Wenvoe, then the only up train of the day, although there was a 6.55pm from Barry Island on Summer Saturdays. The carriage sidings were taken out of use in 1963 and the bay followed in 1972. (G.Adams/M.J.Stretton)

24.   Seen from the roadside near Barry Junction box on 27th August 1959 is the 1.0pm Merthyr to Barry Island service, hauled by 0-6-2T no. 5618. It is about to descend at 1 in 80 to the viaduct. The lines to the left of the loco gave access to No. 1 Dock and West Pond triangle, which was used for turning locomotives. (S.P.Derek)

25.   On the left is Barry Junction box, which was in use from 1907 to 11th May 1964 and had a 90-lever frame. The photo was taken shortly after its closure, while the relief lines and their connections were being removed. The engine shed is on the right and the former locomotive works is in the centre distance. (B.P.Mills)

26.   Only two through platforms have been available since 1964 and passing the up one on 21st May 1995 is a diverted Swansea to London HST. Barry Station box had a 101-lever frame, lost its suffix in 1964 and was still in use in 2005. On the right is the approach to the wagon repair shed which was accessed by the connection behind the signal box. This link was still in situ in 2005 for use by the VoGR. (M.J.Stretton)

27.   A new building was completed on 28th March 1955 and the excessive platform width was reduced. The centre signal is for the down goods loop, which begins close to the bridge in this September 2003 view. The signals were replaced by a three-aspect colour light one with feathers in October 2004 and a new double junction with new point rodding was installed. The goods loop was retained. (V.Mitchell)

BARRY - Engine Shed

28.   This was the principal shed of the BR and outside it on 1st May 1927 was no. 1312, formerly BR no. 87, and no. 778, once BR no. 138. They had both been built by Hudswell Clarke. (H.C.Casserley)

29.   The west end was recorded on 31st August 1947 when the shed was coded BRY. It became 88C in 1948 and around 80 locos were allocated here. Steam traction ceased in September 1964. (W.Potter/R.M.Casserley coll.)

30.   Part of the diesel fleet was recorded on 29th August 1971, with the down platform canopy on the right. The left part of the shed was then being used for wagon repairs and it was soon used entirely for that purpose, the diesels being kept in the sidings on the left. The repairing of wagons ceased in 2000 and the building came into the custody of the VoGR. It soon housed "The Barry Ten" mentioned earlier. VoGR trains began using the line on the right in 2004. (D.H.Mitchell)

BARRY - Loco Works

XII.   This map continues from the top of the previous one and includes the goods depot and its six-ton crane. The building appears in picture no. 16. The locomotive works were completed in 1887 and came into use in stages during the 1890s. The Barry had a fleet of 148 mainly British-built engines, only four of which had tenders and they were 0-8-0s. All had a chocolate-crimson livery. The building southwest of the works was for carriage repairs and the one to the east was a hydraulic pumping station. Only this and the goods shed now remain, but the larger part of the latter was demolished, it being a steel-sheeted extension. The VoGR lines approach the goods shed via a new single line incline from the left of it, all lines to the right and below the "Locomotive Repairing Works" having been lifted.

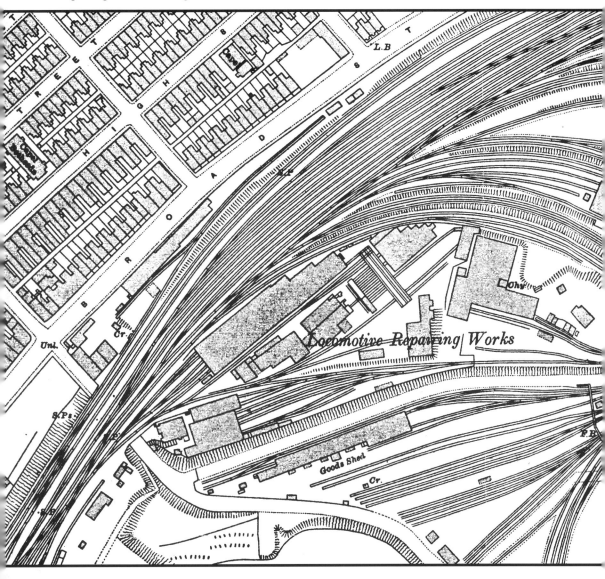

31.   The stones in the gable ends declare "B.R" and "1887". The tracks each side of the right wall continued to a traverser, which gave access to the adjacent buildings. Nos 2168, 1609 and 5668 were in attendance on 21st August 1955. The hut housed ATC (Automatic Train Control) testing equipment; an operating ramp is in the foreground. (B.J.Miller coll.)

32.   The last locomotive left the works on Christmas Eve in 1959, the premises being used for wagon repairs subsequently, until 1962. This view includes a wide range of belt-driven machine tools, together with an overhead crane propelled by the ropes on the right wall. Under repair on 8th May 1959 were nos 5641, 9714, 6644 and 5687. (B.J.Miller coll.)

BARRY DOCKS

33.   An eastward panorama from 1922 has the gasworks and the tall flour mill on the left and countless wagons awaiting movement. The curved sidings branch from the High Level goods lines and pass over the Low Level ones at the waterfront of No. 1 Dock. Most of the coal hoists were replaced later by taller ones, but their description on the maps is indiscriminate. (GWR Magazine)

34.   The gas works was started in 1886 and taken over by Barry Urban District Council in 1896 as the town rapidly expanded under the influence of the new port. Only 2800 tons of coal were carbonised in 1896 but 18,200 tons were used in 1900. Thereafter the coal tonnage remained fairly constant, the added demand being taken up by carburetted water gas. As a result there were plenty of tank wagons in and out of the gas works sidings, with oil demand reaching 517,000 gallons in 1947. The plant struggled to meet demand. Fortunately, the Cardiff Gas Company had a surplus of gas and a connecting main was laid in 1949. Barry thereafter received its gas from Cardiff steel works. (Wales Gas)

35. The north portal of the Graving Dock tunnel was recorded in June 1960 from a passing train, with the station in the right background. Traffic was once so heavy that 100 coal trains would arrive at Cadoxton per day. The short trains from there, plus empties returning, made this flyunder essential. There was only one track after 1964 (the one on the left) and the structure was partially reroofed in 1996 to take the Millennium Way, but the right half was infilled. (M.Dart)

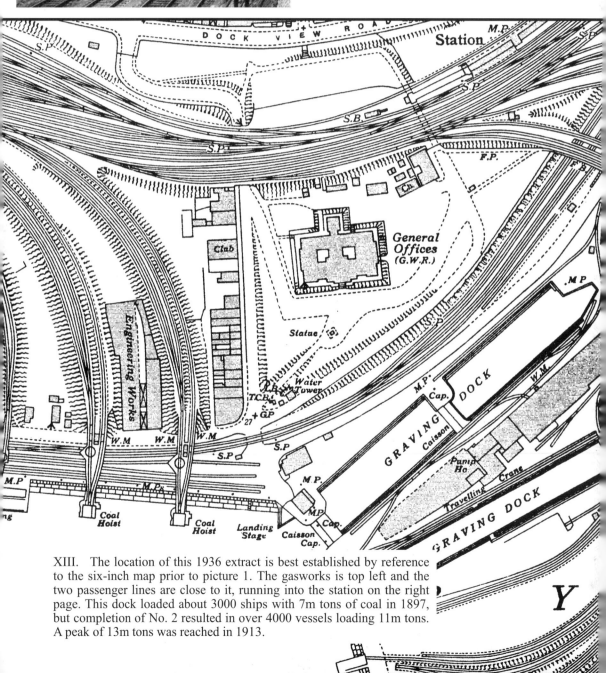

XIII. The location of this 1936 extract is best established by reference to the six-inch map prior to picture 1. The gasworks is top left and the two passenger lines are close to it, running into the station on the right page. This dock loaded about 3000 ships with 7m tons of coal in 1897, but completion of No. 2 resulted in over 4000 vessels loading 11m tons. A peak of 13m tons was reached in 1913.

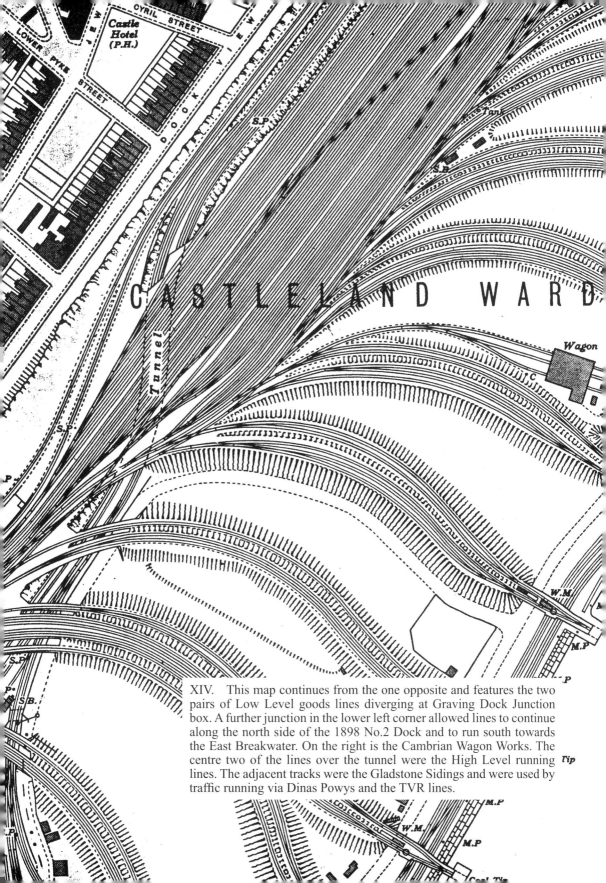

Castle
Hotel
(P.H.)

CYRIL STREET

DOCK VIEW

LOWER PIKE STREET

CASTLELAND WARD

Tunnel

Wagon

S.P.

S.B.

Tank

C

W.M.

M.P

S.B.

S.P.

P

P

Tip

XIV.   This map continues from the one opposite and features the two pairs of Low Level goods lines diverging at Graving Dock Junction box. A further junction in the lower left corner allowed lines to continue along the north side of the 1898 No.2 Dock and to run south towards the East Breakwater. On the right is the Cambrian Wagon Works. The centre two of the lines over the tunnel were the High Level running lines. The adjacent tracks were the Gladstone Sidings and were used by traffic running via Dinas Powys and the TVR lines.

W.M.

M.P

M.P

Coal Tip

36. The platform spans the borders of both of the two previous maps. This westward view from the 1960s includes the 32-lever box, which functioned between 1908 and 1964. The HQ of the BR has the domed clock tower and is shown on map XIII as GWR property. The British Transport Commission took it over in 1948. In 1962 it became the offices of the British Transport Docks Board (later Associated British Ports) and is now occupied by the Vale of Glamorgan Council. There was a traffic staff of 33 at the station in 1923; it is now unstaffed, with one small shelter. (Lens of Sutton coll.)

37. Modern wagon-discharge and conveyor systems were employed in Barry's last effort to export fuel. This southward view of No. 2 Dock is from the late 1970s and has the flour mill in the background. (N.W.Sprinks)

38. A photo from 26th August 1994 features no. 56073 *Tremorfa Steelworks* running along the north side of No.2 Dock, with Barry Island in the distance.The tanks had conveyed vinyl chloride monomer and are about to pass under the 1978 coke conveyor, since demolished, before turning north to pass through the tunnel shown on map XIV. This traffic was transferred to coastal shipping, leaving little activity in the area once busy serving BP Chemicals and Dow Corning. Grain and bananas were once important. (A.Kenny)

39.   Export of coal dwindled during the 1980s, but some phurnacite was despatched using the coke conveyor. However, coal made a brief come back, but only for local use. We see no. 56037 with containers of household coal from Brynteg for W.Baker & Sons on the south side of No. 2 Dock on 1st October 1998. The traffic was short lived, but some chemical containers used part of the quayside line later. (A.Kenny)

CADOXTON

XV.   The 1947 survey at 6ins to 1 mile has the line from Barry lower left, the Wenvoe route above it and the direct route to Cardiff top right. Initially TVR trains from Penarth (lower right) were forced to terminate east of the junction and passengers had to walk "across fields" to reach the BR station. The TVR established a goods depot in this vicinity, but it was closed on 1st April 1925. There were private sidings from it to two brickworks between about 1893 and 1904. The yard was used for wagon repairs by Hall Lewis in 1926-33. Biglis Junction box had 32 levers and closed on 6th May 1951.

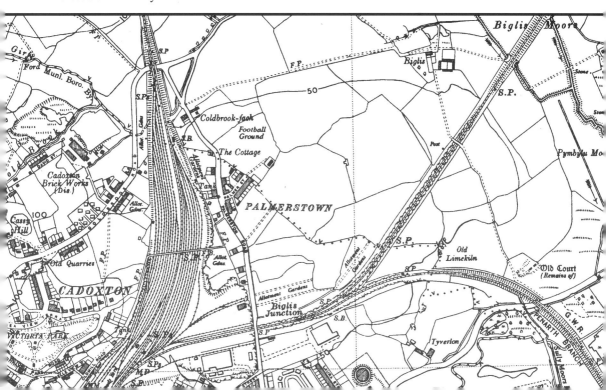

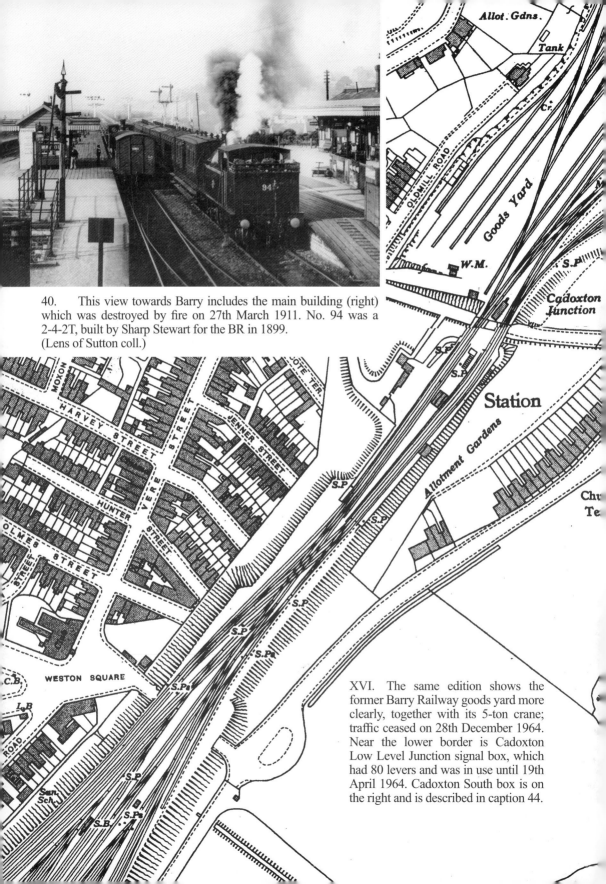

40.   This view towards Barry includes the main building (right) which was destroyed by fire on 27th March 1911. No. 94 was a 2-4-2T, built by Sharp Stewart for the BR in 1899. (Lens of Sutton coll.)

XVI. The same edition shows the former Barry Railway goods yard more clearly, together with its 5-ton crane; traffic ceased on 28th December 1964. Near the lower border is Cadoxton Low Level Junction signal box, which had 80 levers and was in use until 19th April 1964. Cadoxton South box is on the right and is described in caption 44.

41.   The staff peaked here at 80 in 1929, most being concerned with coal traffic. This view in the other direction shows, on the left, the space formerly occupied by the up building. The position of the temporary replacement is shown on map XVI. A brick-built structure was erected in 1954. TVR trains terminated in the platforms on the right. (B.J.Miller coll.)

42.   Development of the massive yard north of the station began in 1897, when the first Cadoxton North box came into use. A new box was built in 1904 astride the two running lines. This photo was taken from it in 1922, but it was replaced in 1924 (due to destruction in a gale) by one east of the lines. It had 54 levers and lasted until 1963. There were 19 up sidings and 18 on the down side. (GWR Magazine)

43.   Loaded wagons stand in the down sidings in July 1959 as we admire the intricacies of the Barry's somersault signals. There were two eastward pointing sidings serving a concrete works for many years. They are marked on map XV. A housing estate now occupies the site. (G.Adams/M.J.Stretton)

44.   Known as "Cadoxton South", the 94-lever frame in this box was taken out of use on 27th July 1969. After total closure of the Wenvoe route in 1963, a short section of the up line was retained for berthing the Penarth shuttle DMU between trips, as seen here. The track was lifted from platform 2 in 1966, but that at No. 1 remained as a down reception line. It was still used by the engineers in 2005. The Penarth service ceased in 1968 and the layover siding was soon lifted. The 1954 building is glimpsed on the left.
(Lens of Sutton coll.)

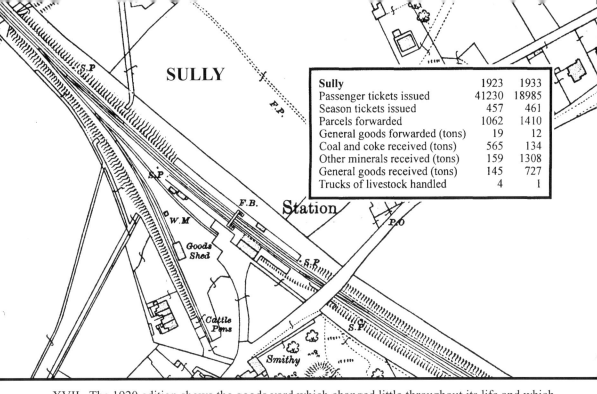

Sully	1923	1933
Passenger tickets issued	41230	18985
Season tickets issued	457	461
Parcels forwarded	1062	1410
General goods forwarded (tons)	19	12
Coal and coke received (tons)	565	134
Other minerals received (tons)	159	1308
General goods received (tons)	145	727
Trucks of livestock handled	4	1

XVII. The 1920 edition shows the goods yard which changed little throughout its life and which was open from 5th November 1888 until 7th October 1963. There was a 5-ton crane listed here in 1938. The"Sully Inn" now occupies the building shown as "Smithy".

45. There were seldom crowds of this magnitude as the population rose from only 175 in 1901 to 722 in 1961. The signal box in the background had a 20-lever frame and closed on 29th January 1965. (Lens of Sutton coll.)

46.   Seen from Cog Road on 9th October 1966, total closure was two years away. There had been five employees here from 1923 to 1938, but there was none after 10th October 1966. The lighting was always by oil. Modern housing and a British Telecom Depot now occupy the site. (B.P.Mills)

SWANBRIDGE HALT

47.   Another view from 9th October 1966, but this is eastwards. This was the most southerly point on the loop and was ½ mile south of Cog. Behind the camera were two steep paths down to the lane to Swanbridge. The platforms were opened in 1906 and extended in 1917. (B.P.Mills)

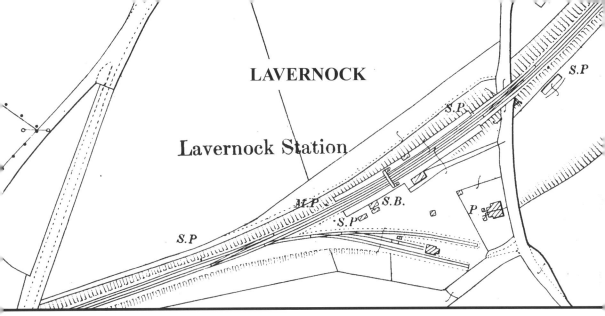

LAVERNOCK

Lavernock Station

XVIII. The 1900 survey shows a footpath up from the lane to the nearby village which grew from 118 souls to 126 over a period of 60 years. There were two men recorded here, presumably to cover two shifts, a lonely location indeed. The goods yard closed on 7th October 1963 and the signal box (S.B.) followed on 29th January 1965. Its frame had just 16 levers.

Lavernock	1923	1933
Passenger tickets issued	19017	10961
Season tickets issued	76	71
Parcels forwarded	831	217
General goods forwarded (tons)	20	6
Coal and coke received (tons)	20	8
Other minerals received (tons)	65	16
General goods received (tons)	150	18
Trucks of livestock handled	-	-

48.   The main building was similar to the one at Sully, but devoid of a canopy and a little shorter. Part of one platform was still intact in 2004. This view towards Penarth is from the early 1960s, when there was still a crossover near the bridge parapets in the distance. The up distant signal is that of Penarth Cement Works box. (Lens of Sutton coll.)

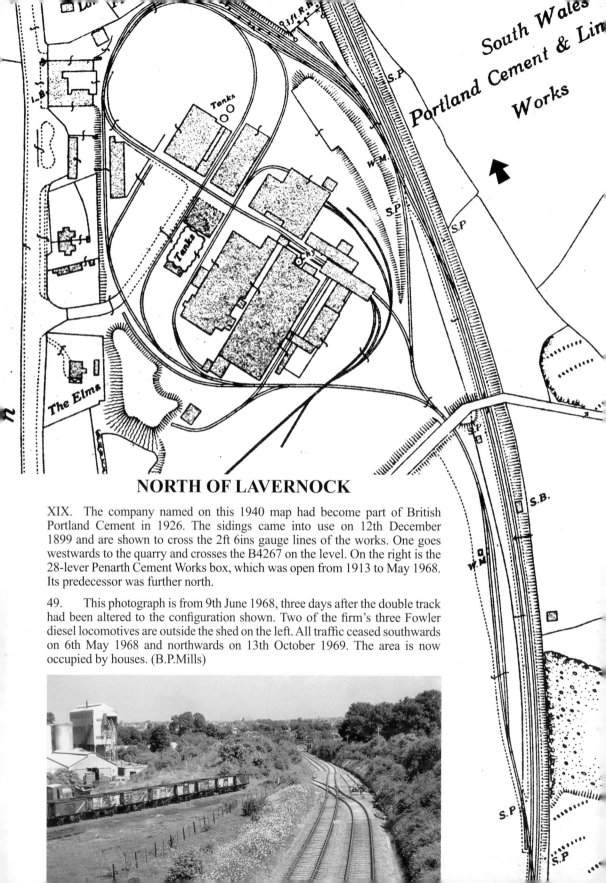

NORTH OF LAVERNOCK

XIX. The company named on this 1940 map had become part of British Portland Cement in 1926. The sidings came into use on 12th December 1899 and are shown to cross the 2ft 6ins gauge lines of the works. One goes westwards to the quarry and crosses the B4267 on the level. On the right is the 28-lever Penarth Cement Works box, which was open from 1913 to May 1968. Its predecessor was further north.

49.   This photograph is from 9th June 1968, three days after the double track had been altered to the configuration shown. Two of the firm's three Fowler diesel locomotives are outside the shed on the left. All traffic ceased southwards on 6th May 1968 and northwards on 13th October 1969. The area is now occupied by houses. (B.P.Mills)

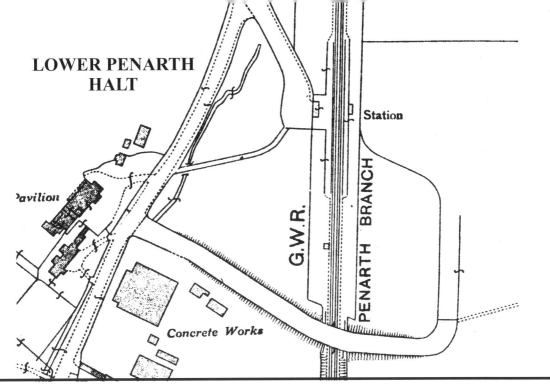

LOWER PENARTH HALT

Pavilion

Concrete Works

Station

G.W.R.

PENARTH BRANCH

XX.   This 1940 map and includes a bridge to take a road to a housing estate that would be many decades coming. It is now Brockhill Rise. There was no access to the down platform from the east side.

50.   The station opened on 1st February 1897, the main building being a great distance from the platform edge, as shown here and on the map. Traffic was poor and the station was downgraded to an unstaffed halt in February 1934 and closed on 14th June 1954. Taken before that date, this photograph includes the foot crossing and also the DC power station with its wooden cooling tower. (Lens of Sutton coll.)

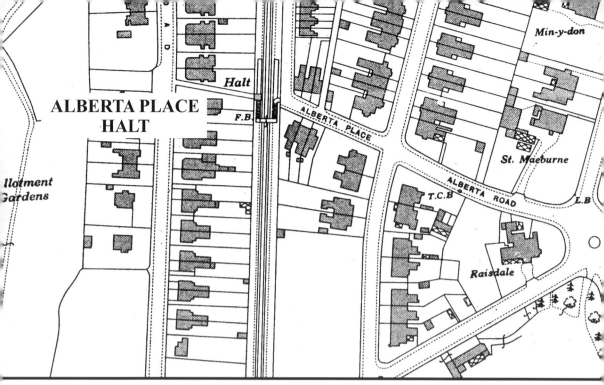

ALBERTA PLACE HALT

XXI. The halt opened on 19th September 1904 for the TVR railmotor service and remained in use until service withdrawal in 1968. It was almost ½ mile from Penarth and is featured on the 1940 edition.

51.   A northward view in the early 1960s reveals modern flat bottom rail. The trackbed remains clear in this vicinity and was considered for the relaying of about one mile of track in 1987, but local opposition prevailed. (B.J.Miller coll.)

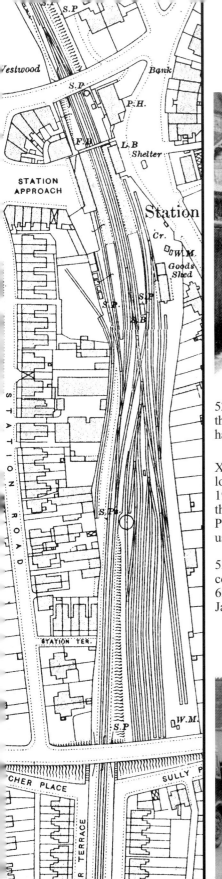

PENARTH

52.   This Edwardian postcard features the a public house (right), the down side building being largely obscured by trees. It appears to have been the earlier of the two. (Lens of Sutton coll.)

XXII. The 1920 edition shows the layout at its optimum with six long carriage sidings. The 30ft turntable was in place between about 1905 and 1925. There was only one platform until April 1889 and that was on the east side of the single line, which was doubled to Penarth Dock on 16th January 1893. The carriage sidings were not used after 1959; their buffers were high above the running lines.

53.   The main entrance became the one on the up side. It was completed in 1890 and photographed in 1952. The staff numbered 63 in 1923, falling to 39 in 1938. The suffix "Town" was used until January 1962. (Lens of Sutton coll.)

54. The middle road was signalled for up movements, such as locos of terminating trains which had been uncoupled by a man standing on the boards in the foreground. The buffers of both bay platforms are visible; these were available for use from 1889 until 1959, but saw few passengers. At the far end of the down platform was North Box, which was in use in 1889-93.
(Lens of Sutton coll.)

55. On the left is the goods shed; all such traffic ceased on 4th April 1966. The back-to-back buffer stops at the up platform allowed the shuttle train from Cadoxton to use the same platform as the Cardiff terminating trains. This applied from 13th February 1967, when the down line was abandoned and the middle road served only the cement works. The signal box which had 56 levers, closed on 6th May 1968, when the Cadoxton service ceased.
(B.J.Miller coll.)

56. The line to the cement works closed in 1969 leaving only a single line to be photographed in September 2003. A new building was completed in December 1974 and the ticket office was open on workday mornings. A cycle store was added in 1987. The population rose from 2652 in 1871 to 11,103 in 1901, 20,890 in 1961 and 22,316 in 2001.
(V.Mitchell)

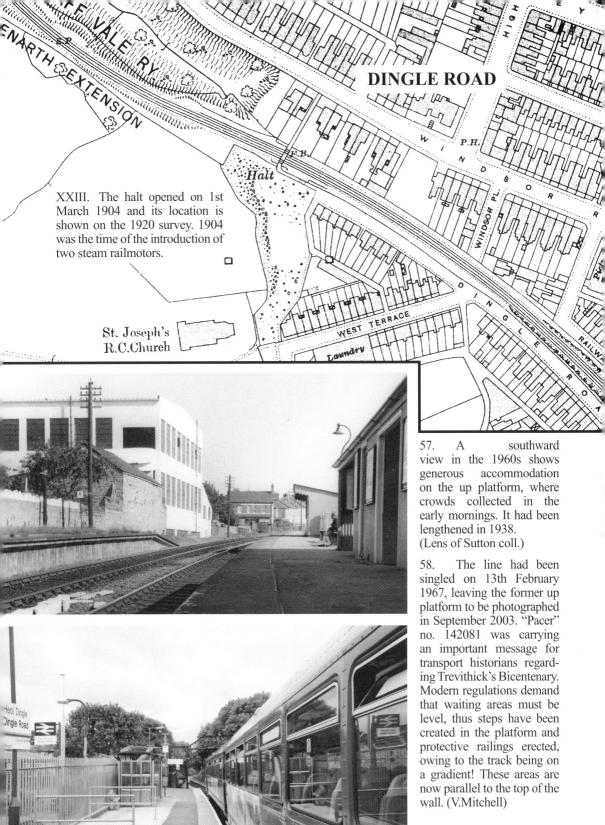

DINGLE ROAD

XXIII. The halt opened on 1st March 1904 and its location is shown on the 1920 survey. 1904 was the time of the introduction of two steam railmotors.

St. Joseph's R.C.Church

57. A southward view in the 1960s shows generous accommodation on the up platform, where crowds collected in the early mornings. It had been lengthened in 1938. (Lens of Sutton coll.)

58. The line had been singled on 13th February 1967, leaving the former up platform to be photographed in September 2003. "Pacer" no. 142081 was carrying an important message for transport historians regarding Trevithick's Bicentenary. Modern regulations demand that waiting areas must be level, thus steps have been created in the platform and protective railings erected, owing to the track being on a gradient! These areas are now parallel to the top of the wall. (V.Mitchell)

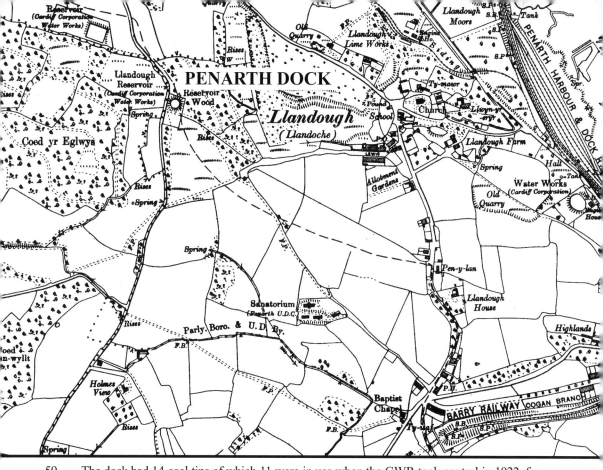

59.   The dock had 14 coal tips of which 11 were in use when the GWR took control in 1922, four of them accepting 20-ton wagons. There were also nine hydraulic cranes. Trade declined and only four tips were functional when the dock was requisitioned for wartime purposes in 1940. It closed in 1963, but most of the sidings had been lifted in 1955. It is seen in about 1883 and is now a marina. The coal exported in 1923 amounted to 3.4m tons, but it was down to 2.5m in 1927 and further decline followed. (B.J.Miller coll.)

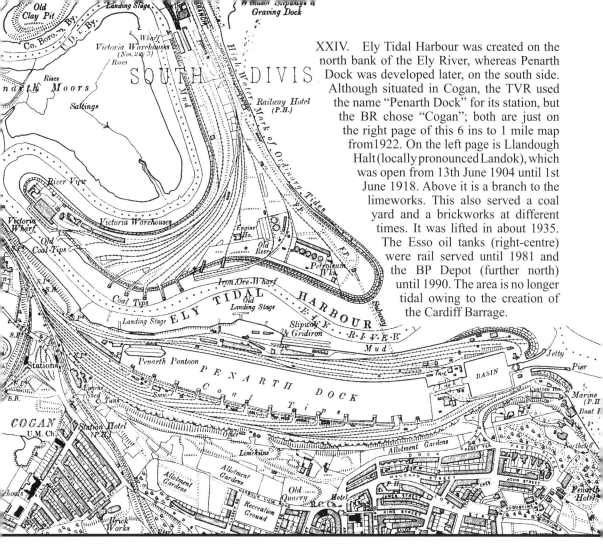

XXIV. Ely Tidal Harbour was created on the north bank of the Ely River, whereas Penarth Dock was developed later, on the south side. Although situated in Cogan, the TVR used the name "Penarth Dock" for its station, but the BR chose "Cogan"; both are just on the right page of this 6 ins to 1 mile map from 1922. On the left page is Llandough Halt (locally pronounced Landok), which was open from 13th June 1904 until 1st June 1918. Above it is a branch to the limeworks. This also served a coal yard and a brickworks at different times. It was lifted in about 1935. The Esso oil tanks (right-centre) were rail served until 1981 and the BP Depot (further north) until 1990. The area is no longer tidal owing to the creation of the Cardiff Barrage.

60.   This was the only intermediate station on the Penarth branch, when it came into use on 20th February 1878. The station closed on 1st January 1962; it had no public goods facilities. Photographed soon after closure, the main building was still standing in 2005, in commercial use and with additions. In the background is Cogan Junction signal box. (Lens of Sutton coll.)

61.　　The GWR box opened on 19th September 1926, but the 1889 TVR box was retained behind it as a store and workshop. Photographed in 1957, operation ceased on 13th February 1967. The frame had 70 levers. Thereafter there was one track southwards, two westwards and four northwards, albeit only as far as the viaduct. The signal box at the south end of Cogan platform closed in 1926. It had 22 levers and was replaced by a ground frame. (P.J.Garland/R.S.Carpenter)

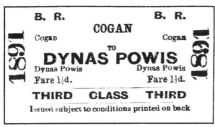

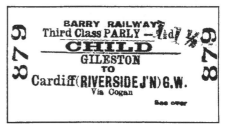

62.   The location is Llandough Sidings and is near the top of the left page of map XXIV where a tank is marked. TVR class V 0-6-0ST no. 99 is shunting on 24th July 1922. The maximum number of sidings here was 18. There was a signal box at each end of them between 1903 and 1936: Llandough Upper and Llandough Lower. There was just one until 1966. (R.S.Carpenter coll.)

63.   The Ely Viaduct was recorded on 28th November 1959, after an 0-6-0PT with the 2.33pm Cardiff General to Penarth Town had passed an 0-6-2T. The bowstring structure was removed in 1966; it carried only the up main line. (S.P.Derek)

GRANGETOWN

XXV. The 1922 survey at 6 ins to 1 mile has the Ely Viaduct lower left, there being three tracks on the eastern span and one on the other. The route lower right is for Ely Tidal Dock and was from 1859. The gasworks is south of the junction, the station being close to it. North thereof is Penarth South Junction, the right side of the triangle being provided for TVR trains to gain access to Cardiff (top right), the left side being used mainly by their coal trains. Above the triangle is Canton engine shed and the GWR main line. This map continues from no. XXIV, the Taff Wagon Works being partly on both. Ninian Park Halt is top left.

64.   The station opened on 29th May 1882 and its two platforms were replaced by an island one in 1904. A TVR I class 4-4-0T is sandwiched between two of their 1907 autocoaches at the down platform. The goods lines are in the foreground. There was a staff of 56 in 1929-30, but it was 34 in the late 1930s. (Lens of Sutton coll.)

65.   The Cardiff Gas Light & Coke Company's works began production in 1865, expanded over the Grangetown Iron Works site in 1887 and continued to grow until it was the largest in Wales. The sidings were rebuilt with an inclined plane into the coal stores in 1893 and extended on two levels in 1907. A narrow-gauge coke tramway, manually-powered, had lift-off wagon bodies; a gantry steam crane emptied them to create high storage heaps, or into bunkers. Coke from the bunkers was railed to Cardiff Docks for export. Yorkshire coal was used, 18,200 tons in 1900, for example. It came by 2500-ton steamers to Penarth and on by rail to Grangetown. Later plant was able to use a growing proportion of South Wales coal. The GWR gasworks in Cardiff ceased making gas for Bute Docks around 1940, which added to Grangetown's load. Coal consumption here reached 106,000 tons in 1938, but dropped to a fraction in 1947 when coke-oven gas became available from Guest Keen's Cardiff steel works. The photo is from the 1950s and gas output more than doubled in the 1960s, but this was not coal, but oil-based. A shortage of rail tank wagons meant that butane feedstock had to be shipped from Ireland in 1963-64, but as soon as the rolling stock could be built, 300-ton lots of butane by rail became regular. These were quickly followed by special trains of LDF (also called PFD; really just petrol) which each delivered 500 tons of feedstock. The discovery of North Sea gas put an end to this traffic and production ceased in November 1972. (Wales Gas)

66.   A northward view from the 1960s reveals the generous weather protection provided at this populous location. In the distance on the left is the 75-lever Penarth Curve South box, which was in use from 1915 to 1966. (Lens of Sutton coll.)

67.   The 17.38 Penarth to Cardiff Queen Street was recorded on 22nd October 1982, by which time the buildings had been demolished due to destaffing. The once-roofed stairway is on the left. A waiting shed sufficed for many years, but in 2004 a new unbelievably passenger-hostile roof-only shelter appeared at this very windswept location, a deterrent indeed! (T.Heavyside)

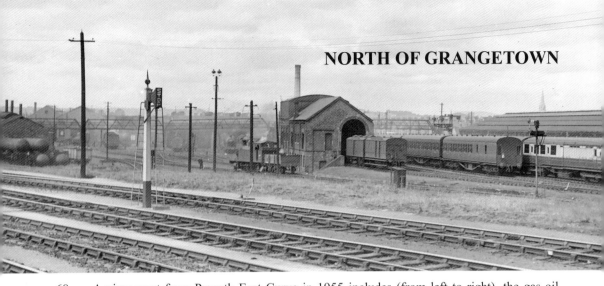

68.   A view west from Penarth East Curve in 1955 includes (from left to right), the gas oil works (once it provided fuel for carriage lighting, but by then only for dining car cookers), Canton Engine Shed of 1882 (engulfed in smoke haze as usual), the coal stage (surmounted by a water tank) and carriage sidings, beyond which are the main lines and the 1899 carriage shed, which became a milk depot prior to 1934. The engine shed closed to steam traction in September 1962. (S.Rickard/B.J.Miller coll.)

69.   A class 116 DMU is bound for Barry on 28th March 1976 and is running alongside the two up tracks of Penarth Curve East. The diesels were stabled in the open, as the sheds were used for their servicing from October 1963. (T.Heavyside)

CARDIFF CENTRAL

70.   The station was extensively rebuilt in 1876-77. As elsewhere, the GWR employed the suffix "General" for its principal station in the city; it was in use from 1st July 1924. A major rebuild in 1933 resulted in this elegant north facade. The main entrance is seen in about 1960. (S.P.Derek)

71.   The curved platforms south of the main station were used by Barry trains from 14th August 1893. The platforms were termed "Riverside" until 28th October 1940, when they became platforms 8 and 9. In the background is no. 7 which, along with no. 6, was used by TVR trains between Penarth and Queen Street from 1st February 1883. Clarence Road station closed on 16th March 1964, after which time nos 8 and 9 were used mostly for mail, this railtour on 8th October 1983 being an exception. (D.H.Mitchell)

72.   Platform 6 is on the left as no. 67013 runs east with a mail train, the service being in terminal decline. The view from 10th September 2003 includes an example of the 1933 architecture. Platform 5 had been a bay at the west end until 1965; the number was not used subsequently. (V.Mitchell)

73.   A "Pacer" stands at platform 7 on the same day as we examine the south entrance. The left gable end also appears in picture 71. Platforms 8 and 9 were removed in 1993, the branch having been taken out of use in July 1968. The present panel box was built near its junction and opened on 21st March 1966. (V.Mitchell)

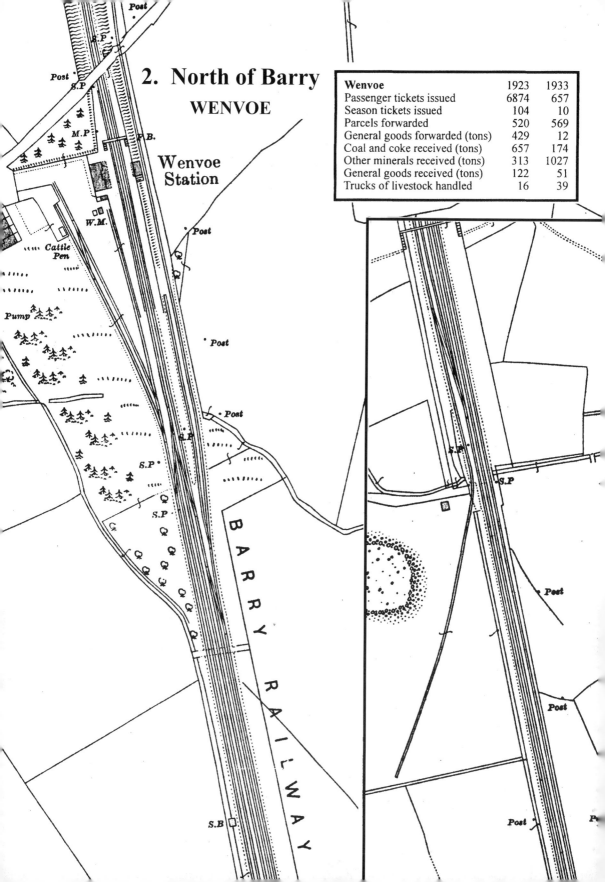

2. North of Barry

WENVOE

Wenvoe
Station

Wenvoe	1923	1933
Passenger tickets issued	6874	657
Season tickets issued	104	10
Parcels forwarded	520	569
General goods forwarded (tons)	429	12
Coal and coke received (tons)	657	174
Other minerals received (tons)	313	1027
General goods received (tons)	122	51
Trucks of livestock handled	16	39

BARRY RAILWAY

(left) XXVI. The inset section on the right continues from the main map, which is from 1920. The line from Cadoxton Yard rose at 1 in 127 for two miles to a level section south of the station. Lower left on the inset section is a siding serving a reservoir, built to supply the Barry Dock complex. At the top of the main map, the running lines pass under a road, whereas a siding passes over it on the level to serve Alps Quarry. At the bottom is the 31-lever signal box and 1¼ miles to the south was St. Andrews Box, until about 1950.

74. A passenger service was provided here from 16th March 1896 until 10th September 1962, although the population was only 489 in 1901. The building became a desirable residence after line closure. The photo is probably from the 1920s. (B.J.Miller coll.)

75. On the right of this southward view is the small goods yard, which closed on 2nd December 1963 with the route. The track behind the camera is running downhill at 1 in 400 towards the 1868yd-long Wenvoe Tunnel. One of the two down sidings can be seen on the left, at a high level. The two loops south of the platforms were level and remained to the end. The map omits the southern crossover on the down side. (B.P.Mills)

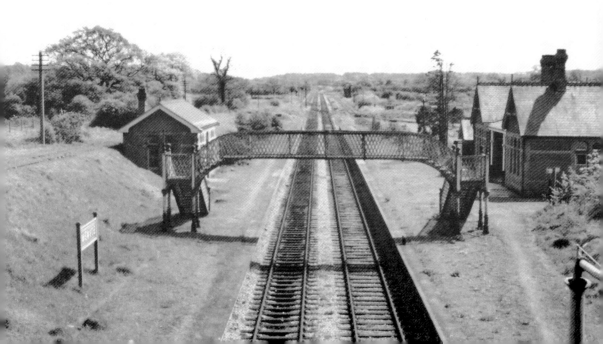

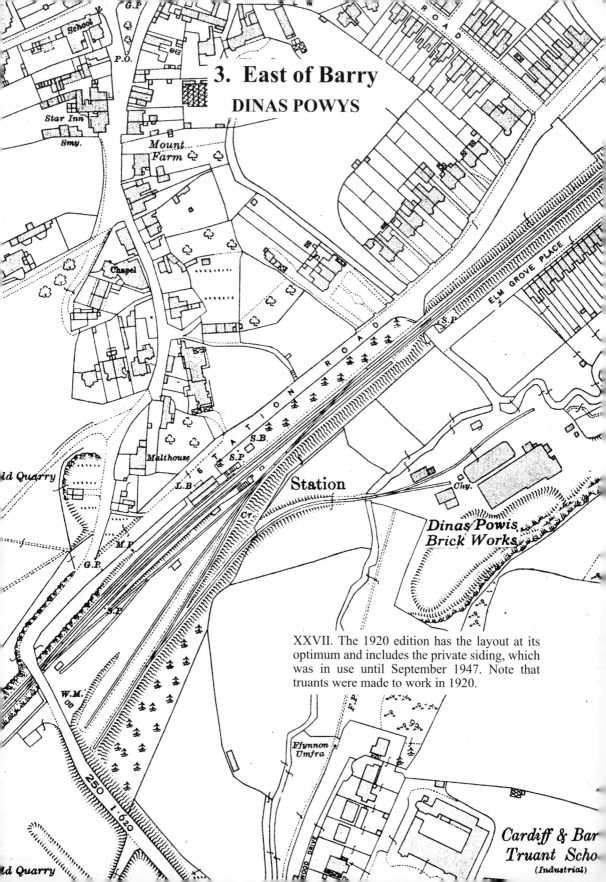

3. East of Barry
DINAS POWYS

XXVII. The 1920 edition has the layout at its optimum and includes the private siding, which was in use until September 1947. Note that truants were made to work in 1920.

76.   Another double-stripe somersault signal is evident as BR class J 2-4-2T no. 94 waits with a down train in about 1912. The goods yard was in use until 1st April 1963. (Lens of Sutton coll.)

77.   A September 1953 record includes the 27-lever signal box, which closed on 14th December 1962. The Morris Minor is from the early low headlamp era. (Lens of Sutton coll.)

78.   This eastward view is from the late 1960s. The staff level reduced from 12 to 9 during the 1930s and manning ceased on 2nd February 1970. Demolition followed and gas lighting ended. Brick-built shelters came next to be superseded by glass and steel structures. (Lens of Sutton coll.)

79.   Total renovation was completed on 30th September 1985 and is seen on 18th December 2004, as EWS no. 66220 runs west with coal for Aberthaw Power Station. There is a subway between the platforms, which were rebuilt devoid of ramps. (N.W.Sprinks)

EASTBROOK

80.   To create a "park & ride" facility and to serve fresh housing development in the village of Eastbrook, a new station was opened on 24th November 1986, ¾ mile east of Dinas Powys. The class 116 unit was nearing the end of its life when photographed on 14th July 1988 working the 12.52 Barry Island to Caerphilly service. (N.W.Sprinks)

COGAN

81.   In the centre background is Ely Tidal Harbour, while Penarth Dock is on the right. The location is shown on map XXIV, above pictures 59 and 60. Part of the TVR's Penarth Dock station is also included in the middle distance; it is shown more fully in pictures 60-61. (Lens of Sutton coll.)

82.   A view towards Barry in the early 1960s includes several gas lamps. The staff dropped from 14 in 1923 to 7 in 1935. Trains from Barry terminated here for the first few years, passengers having to walk to the TVR station if they were bound for Cardiff. Coal wagons stand in the goods yard, which closed on 2nd November 1964. (Lens of Sutton coll.)

83.   Cogan Junction had limited visibility, as confirmed by this July 1957 photograph. The signals were controlled by the box seen in picture no. 61. There was limited opportunity to overrun them safely. The arms on the left are 5ft long, while those on the right are 4ft. (P.J.Garland/R.S.Carpenter)

84.   After staffing ceased in February 1970, these simple shelters were provided, but the footbridge had to be retained. Less hospitable shelters have followed. Behind the camera is the 223yd long Cogan Tunnel, which penetrates the north-south limestone ridge on which the Penarth Cement Works was situated. (N.W.Sprinks)

(top right) 85.Cogan Junction is on the left and the A4055 viaduct is in the background, as is part of Ely Tidal Harbour. The 10.47 Treherbert to Penarth was being operated by a class 150 on 8th April 1992. This class had been introduced to the area in September 1987. These "Sprinters" were largely displaced by four-wheeled "Pacers" of class 142 and 143 in November 1991. Both goods loops were still in place north of the junction in 2005. The viaduct carries Cogan Spur Road, which was opened on 2nd November 1988. (N.W.Sprinks)

4. West of Barry

86.   Porthkerry Viaduct is 374 yds in length and was a major problem to its builders. As usual, borings were undertaken to determine the depth of solid rock, but, unknown to them, there was a strata of clay under this which gave way below three piers at the Barry end, five weeks after opening. A 2½-mile single track diversion inland was opened three months later. It was more than three years before reconstruction was complete. Revenue loss was enormous and the expected heavy coal traffic from the Bridgend area never did materialise, owing to development of docks at Port Talbot. No. 37181 is westbound on 5th March 1977 with an LNER Society Special destined for the Central Wales line. There had been a private halt for Lord Romilly at the west end of the structure in the early years. Porthkerry Tunnel No. 1 is to the east and is 545 yds long; No. 2 is 71 yds and to the west. (N.W.Sprinks)

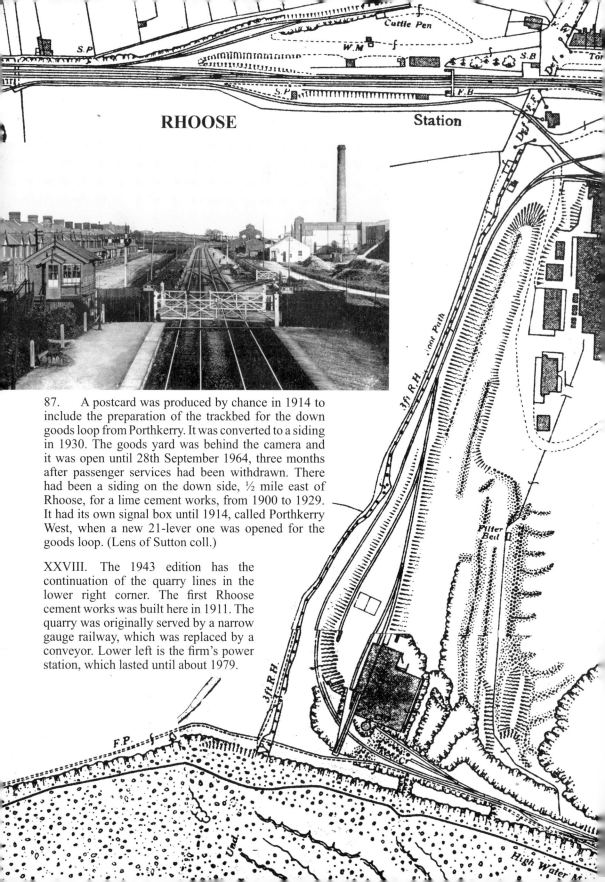

RHOOSE

Station

87. A postcard was produced by chance in 1914 to include the preparation of the trackbed for the down goods loop from Porthkerry. It was converted to a siding in 1930. The goods yard was behind the camera and it was open until 28th September 1964, three months after passenger services had been withdrawn. There had been a siding on the down side, ½ mile east of Rhoose, for a lime cement works, from 1900 to 1929. It had its own signal box until 1914, called Porthkerry West, when a new 21-lever one was opened for the goods loop. (Lens of Sutton coll.)

XXVIII. The 1943 edition has the continuation of the quarry lines in the lower right corner. The first Rhoose cement works was built here in 1911. The quarry was originally served by a narrow gauge railway, which was replaced by a conveyor. Lower left is the firm's power station, which lasted until about 1979.

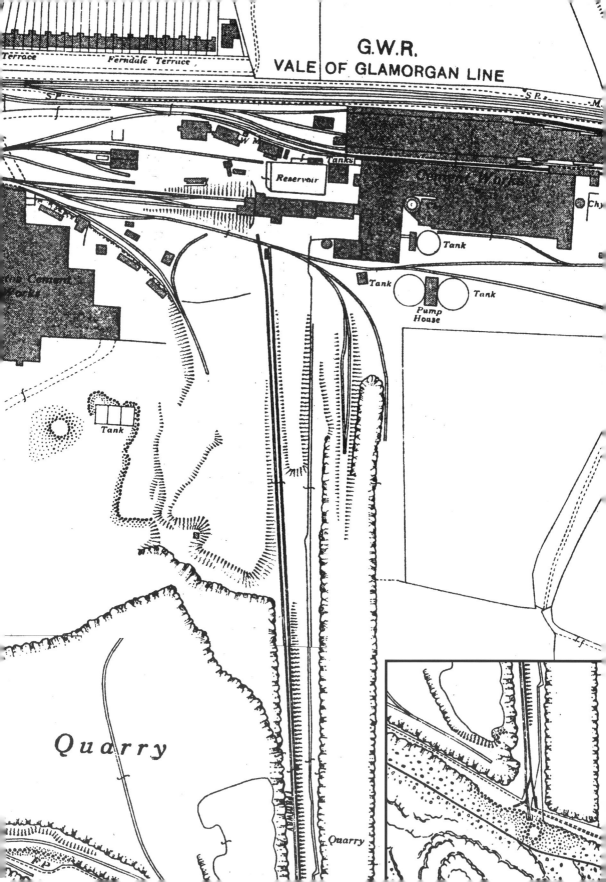

Terrace   Ferndale Terrace

G.W.R.
VALE OF GLAMORGAN LINE

S.P.   S.P.   M.

Reservoir

Tanks

Cement Works

Chy.

Tank

Tank

Pump
House

Tank

Cement
Works

Tank

Quarry

Quarry

F.P.

88. This is the approach to the up side building in 1953. It had been extended to the left of the pole in 1916 owing to an increase in traffic associated with expansion of the cement works. The staff rose from two in 1910 to five in 1916.
(Lens of Sutton coll.)

89. An eastward view from the late 1960s includes the gable end of the 24-lever signal box, which was in use until 30th September 1978, when lifting barriers replaced the gates. A ground frame controlled access to the cement works until its closure in 1984.
(Lens of Sutton coll.)

90. The nearby war-time airfield gradually developed for civilian use and UK internal flights increased. It ultimately became Cardiff International Airport and reopening of the station would reduce road traffic by providing a train service to valleys north of Cardiff, plus connections at Bridgend. Unlike its predecessor, the station would have its up platform east of the level crossing, the only one on the route. This is the state of progress on 13th January 2005. (Vale of Glamorgan Council/R.Williams)

ABERTHAW

XXIX. The solitary building to the left of the quadruple track was the low-level terminus of the TVR line from Cowbridge. It opened on 1st October 1892, closing to passengers on 5th May 1930 and to goods on 1st November 1932. The line continued south to Aberthaw Lime Works (1888-1926). The map is from 1943. The goods yard on the right shut on 7th October 1963.

Baptist Chapel

S.P

S.P

S.P

Blue Anchor
(P.H.)

Ty-uchaf

East Aberthaw

P.O.
T.C.B.
Mission
Room

Station

W.M.

F.B.

S.B.

Goods Shed

M.P.

S.P.

S.P.

91. A view towards Barry in July 1959 shows the standard Vale of Glamorgan buildings and well spaced platforms, the centre lines being intended mainly for coal trains. The name "Aberthaw High Level" was used from 1st July 1924 until 7th May 1945. (R.M.Casserley)

92. A panorama in the other direction from 13th July 1957 includes two of the new sidings laid in connection with the construction of Aberthaw 'A' Power Station. The signal box had 53 levers and was the only one between Barry and the Bridgend area still to be in use in 2005. It was known as "Aberthaw East" until 1962. (P.J.Garland/R.S.Carpenter)

93.   From the same bridge on 22nd October 1982, we see no. 47235 with empties, while three of the four reception roads contain loaded wagons waiting entry to the power station. Much of the traffic was on the Merry-go-Round system from December 1971, when Aberthaw 'B' opened. Cement wagons are in the centre; these two sidings were added in 1920. The up loop was taken out of use in 1966. (T.Heavyside)

94.   Looking east from the same bridge on 23rd September 1980, we witness the passage of no. 47242 over the power station junction, which was fully functional from 23rd July 1961. The bridge had been lengthened prior to this. The right track was taken out of use on 22nd August 1981. (D.H.Mitchell)

95.   The Monmouth-
shire Railway Society's
"Coed Bach Connection"
on 8th October 1983 gave
a rare opportunity to see
the private sidings. The
solid fuel is pulverised
and old colliery waste
tips have been burnt,
along   with   Welsh
river dredgings, by the
addition of oil, hence the
tankers right of centre.
The short train left of
centre is in the cripple
siding. (D.H.Mitchell)

96.   Two photographs
in poor weather from
26th September 1994
show   the   revised
layout. Leading is no.
37887 *Castell Caerffili/
Caerphilly Castle* with
no. 37802 following on a
train from Cwmbargoed.
On the left is the disused
'A' station   and   the
multi-flued stack of 'B'
station is on the right.
The trestled structure
supports the exhaust
stacks of the auxiliary
gas turbine. (A.Kenny)

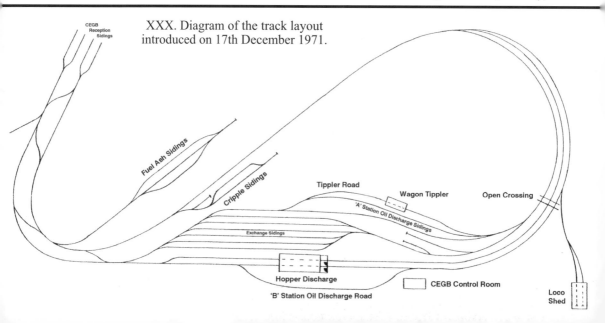

XXX. Diagram of the track layout
introduced on 17th December 1971.

97.   Another view of the same train includes the hopper discharge, beyond which is the control panel building. Trains are limited to 2mph here. 'A' station has subsequently been demolished. The locos are on No. 8 Merry-go-Round line. No. 9 is to the right of them, while nos. 7 and 6 exchange sidings are to the left. Nos 1 to 5 were lifted. (A.Kenny)

98.   A different angle two days later shows the two oil discharge sidings which are connected to the Merry-go-Round route. Only one was used regularly. No. 37906 is in charge of a train from Cardiff Tidal. The station was built specifically for burning South Wales coal, which has over the years been sourced from Blaenant Colliery (now closed and demolished), Cwmbargoed (currently mothballed), Cwmgwrach (still running), Deep Navigation Colliery (now closed and demolished), Merthyr Vale Colliery (now closed and demolished), Onllwyn (still running), Taff Merthyr Colliery (now closed and demolished), Steel Supply (mothballed) and Tower Colliery (still running), to name but a few. Recently however, with the decimation of the South Wales coalfields, imported coal has been used coming from variously Swansea Docks, Port Talbot Grange and Newport Docks, as well as Portbury Docks, the Avonmouth Bulk Handling Terminal and Avonmouth Bennetts. The flows are constantly changing. In November 2004, an average of 69 coal trains arrived per week. (A.Kenny)

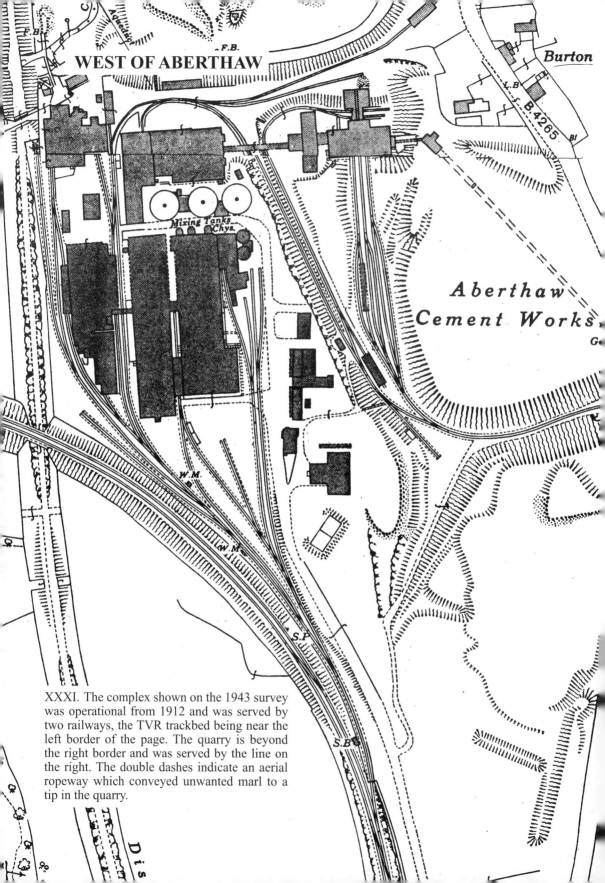

WEST OF ABERTHAW

Burton

Aberthaw Cement Works

Mixing Tanks
Chys.

XXXI. The complex shown on the 1943 survey was operational from 1912 and was served by two railways, the TVR trackbed being near the left border of the page. The quarry is beyond the right border and was served by the line on the right. The double dashes indicate an aerial ropeway which conveyed unwanted marl to a tip in the quarry.

99.   This northward view was taken between the station and the cement works, the chimneys of which are in the background. The power station tracks are on the left and those of the main line on the right. The connection between them dates from 23rd July 1961. The signal was removed on 13th August 1962, when Aberthaw West box closed. (B.P.Mills)

100.   Moving further north, we come to the cement works siding and Aberthaw West box. Its 18-lever frame served as a ground frame from August 1962 until September 1980, when a small one was installed on the right. The works ceased to need coal by rail when the oil tanks on the left were installed. Natural gas followed as the fuel. (B.P.Mills)

101.   A view west from one of the oil tanks in 1961 features an 0-6-2T descending to the power station with loaded coal wagons, devoid of vacuum brakes. The second track had only just been completed. (B.P.Mills)

GILESTON

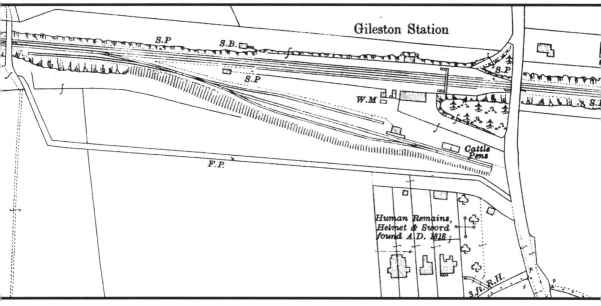

XXXII. The line climbs at 1 in 81 from the Thaw valley through the cutting on the right of this 1919 map. The main coast road passed from St. Athan, over the bridge on the right and through East Aberthaw in the early days.

102.   Gileston (pronounced Jills-tun) housed only 57 souls in 1901, but St. Athan (½ mile to the north) was larger. Further north, one of Britain's largest RAF stations was developed and it used the latter name. (Lens of Sutton coll.)

103.   A 1953 record of the south elevation includes the 21-lever signal box, which was closed on 28th September 1964. Goods traffic ceased on the same day. The gable end on the extreme right is that of a large shelter erected on the up platform for the benefit mainly of RAF personnel. (Lens of Sutton coll.)

104.   An eastward panorama from the early 1960s includes the 1940s up shelter and shows that the signal box had to be high to give a line of sight down the incline beyond the bridge. The station building became an office for a car parking firm. (Lens of Sutton coll.)

ST. ATHAN

XXXIII. The 1943 edition includes the halt which was opened on 1st September 1939 to serve the RAF's West Camp, which often had about 5000 people; East Camp could house more than four times that number and kept Gileston busy. The commencement of the RAF's siding is shown, but the remainder is not, for security reasons. It ran to a coal yard, extensive stores and a locomotive shed until 1969. The 20-lever signal box (top left) was functional from 1938 to 1975, after which time there was no intermediate box between Aberthaw and Bridgend (Cowbridge Road). A link was provided between the box and the airfield control tower.

105.   The halt became a station on 3rd May 1943 and a ticket office was built near the top of the path to the up platform. A roof (left) was provided over part of it to increase the dry waiting area. (Lens of Sutton coll.)

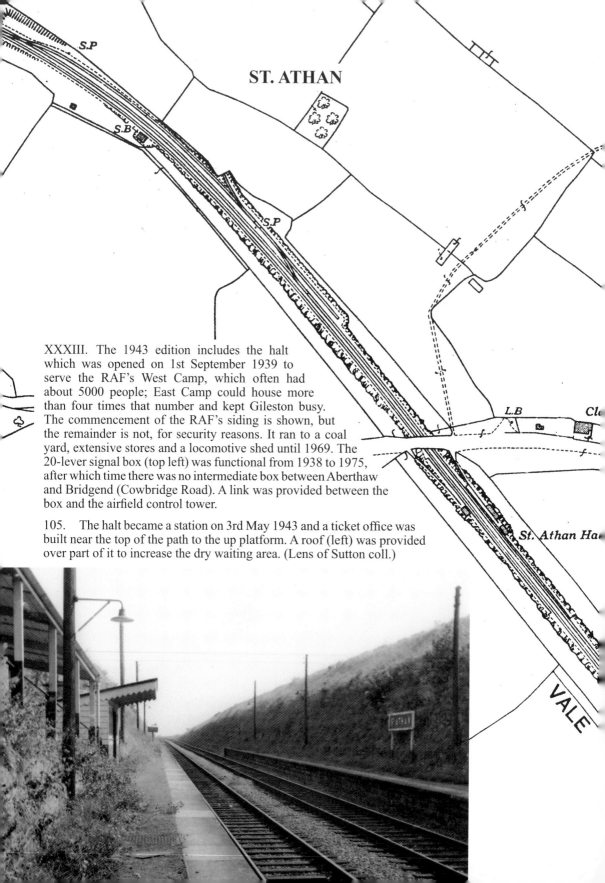

The Mount

Win

LLANTWIT MAJOR

XXXIV. This small town had been a seat of learning since the 6th century but by 1901 it had only 1113 residents. The figure had risen to 4243 by 1961 and 10,791 in 2001. The map is from 1919 and includes two cattle markets created near the station. The town centre is beyond the left border; its name was a corruption of Llanilltrud Fawr. The two short sidings were added in 1900.

S.P

S.P

Bryn Illtya

Llanmaes

Tk.

Auction Mart

Cattle Pens

Station

Cattle Pens

Goods Shed

W.M.

S.P

Boverton Road

+ 157

+ 158

VALE OF GLA

Cattle Pens

Auction Mart

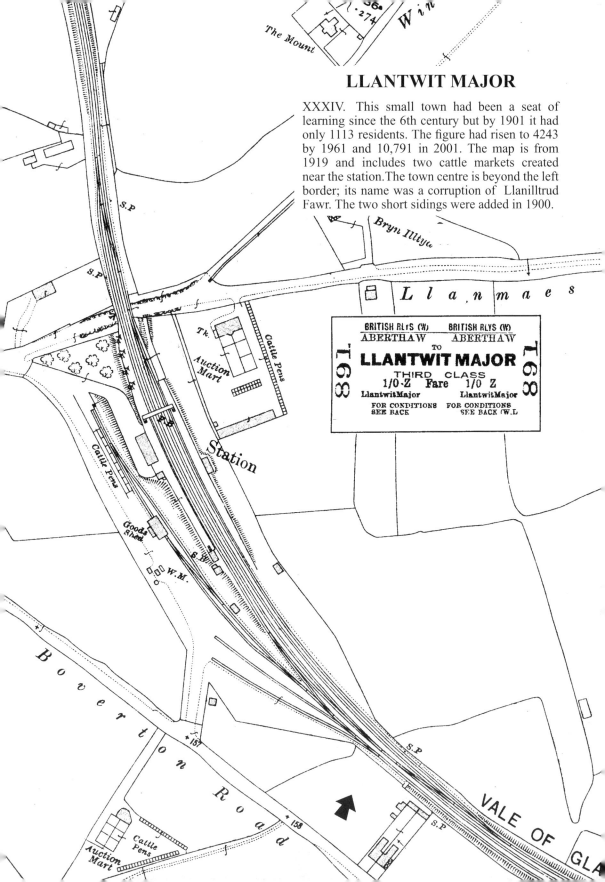

106.   A southward panorama features the 37-lever signal box which was in use until 13th January 1969, when the loops were taken out of use. The goods yard, which was behind it, had closed on 3rd July 1967. An up starting signal was erected at the far end of the down platform in September 1919 to avoid terminating trains having to cross to the up platform for departure. (Lens of Sutton coll.)

107.   This view in the other direction was taken not long after cessation of passenger services in 1964. The arm on the water column was long enough to reach a locomotive standing on the through line. (Lens of Sutton coll.)

108.   The Ford 10 standing near the entrance in 1962 probably belonged to a member of staff, as those with cars at that time seldom used the train. The buildings were demolished in 1968. (Lens of Sutton coll.)

109.   Few would have expected that the station would ever reopen. New platforms were built on the sites of the loops and a new footbridge was positioned on 20th December 2004. (Network Rail)

LLANDOW WICK ROAD HALT

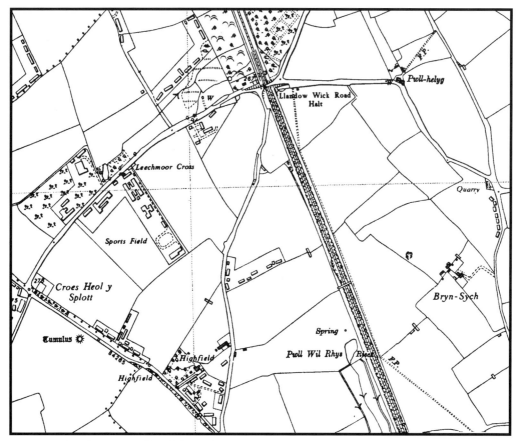

XXXV. The 6ins to 1 mile edition of 1948 indicates the location of the halt in this sparsely populated area.

110. The halt came into use on 19th April 1943 to serve RAF facilities. Standard wartime shelters were provided. The grass covered platforms were photographed in the 1960s when few trains called. (Lens of Sutton coll.)

LLANDOW HALT

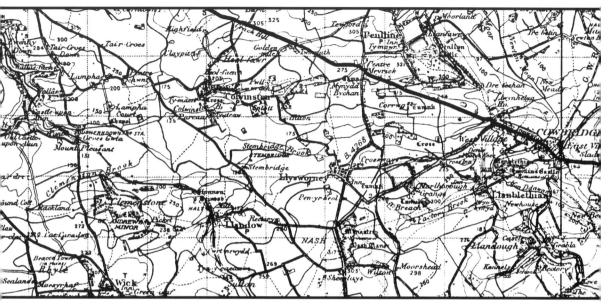

XXXVI. This halt opened on 1st May 1915 and is seen to be close to the village on this 1 ins to 1 mile map of 1947. Also included are the stations at Southerndown Road and Cowbridge.

111.   A northward view from August 1936 includes the lanterns in which the guard would have to place the oil lamps. Limestone strata is visible in the distance. The 15-lever signal box served as a block post and controlled a crossover from November 1898 to November 1959. (B.J.Miller coll.)

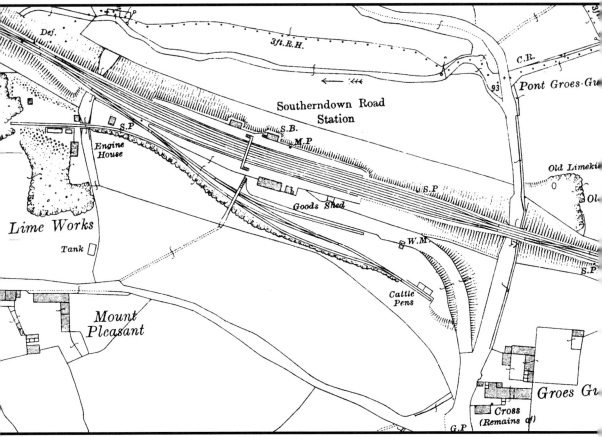

XXXVII. The 1919 survey includes the 1911 private siding for W.H.Morgan's limeworks and the goods shed that was added to the down platform in 1913. Note that there was a footbridge over the goods yard.

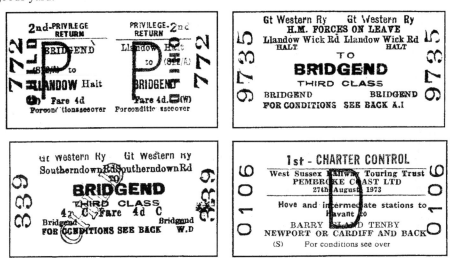

112. The connecting bus to the village was recorded in about 1905, along with the 37-lever signal box. Goods and passenger services were withdrawn on 23rd October 1961, traffic having been very thin in this lightly inhabited region. (Lens of Sutton coll.)

113. This westward view is from the last day of all local traffic and includes the limeworks on the left. The loops and signal box remained in use until 29th March 1967. The footbridge was dismantled at the end of October 1961. (B.P.Mills)

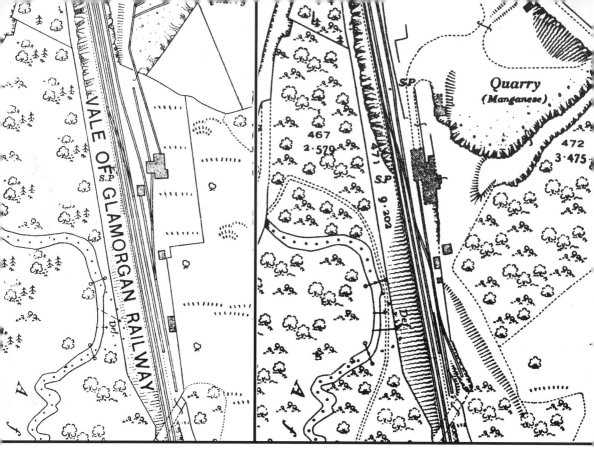

SOUTH OF BRIDGEND

XXXVIII. Almost one mile north of Southerndown Road, there were sidings on the down side for Duchy Quarry (1920-57) and Lancaster Quarry (1928-53). However, these maps are of Ewenny Quarry sidings (1898-1956), which were one mile further north. Left is 1919 and right is 1943. A little further north there was a short siding on the west side for a pumping station (1898-1936). The water was destined for locomotives at Coity Sidings by pipe. The quarries all had small signal boxes.

XXXIX. One mile south of Bridgend, a trailing siding from the up line was added, together with a crossover, on 15th February 1980 to serve Ford's new engine factory. A six-lever ground frame was provided. The diagram shows the layout within the works area, which cannot be visited.

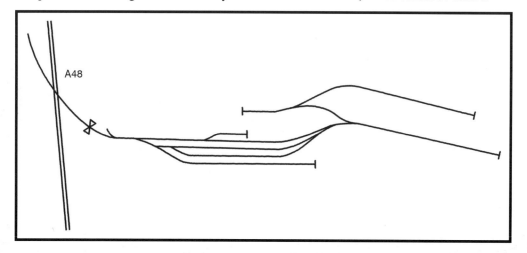

114.   Ford's branch runs westwards for over one mile to their massive factory at Waterton and crosses the A48 on the level. Trains are timed to pass over the road between 05.00 and 06.00 to minimise hold-ups. No. 66112 was running four hours late on 21st July 2000 and was thus recorded in good daylight. A police escort was required on that occasion to protect lawless motorists from their own actions. (A.Kenny)

115.   The trains usually ran at least five days per week and operated between sidings at Dagenham (see map II in *Tilbury Loop*) and Swansea. Train division took place at Bridgend, only part going on to Swansea. Ford's Hudswell Clarke 0-6-0DH (rebuilt by the Yorkshire Engine Co. 1966) was moving empties to the shipping bay on 15th August 1995. Destinations included Halewood and West Germany. (M.J.Stretton)

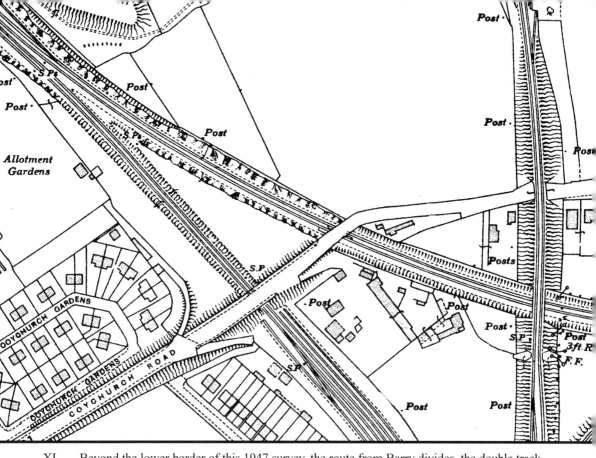

XL.   Beyond the lower border of this 1947 survey, the route from Barry divides, the double track parallel to the right border being the freight-only Bridgend bypass, built by the BR to convey coal via Coity Junction (over one mile to the north) from the Garw and Ogmore Valleys to Barry Docks. It passes over the 1850 main line from Cardiff and diverging from it (top right) is the remnant of a siding that served the Bridgend Lime Company in 1911-36. The double track had become two single lines in May 1938, the eastern one linking two War Department establishments. Lower right is part of a curve to the one at Tremains and also the point at which the freight single track returns to double. The route was double again from about 1950 until closure on 15th June 1964. Lower centre, a drive from Coychurch Road leads down to a short siding, which received public goods inward only from 1st June 1906 until 19th July 1965. It is at the end of the exchange sidings provided for traffic between the BR and the GWR. At their south end was Cowbridge Road Junction, which had a 75-lever frame and was in use until 12th September 1965. It was replaced by Cowbridge Road box, which is still operational (electrically) and near the lower border of the map.

(left) 116. The main line from Cardiff curves in from the left and a train departs for Barry in the distance. The exchange sidings were beyond the bridge. On the right is Bridgend East box, which functioned until 12th September 1965, and the siding for R.S.Hayes Ltd, which lasted until September 1969. This led to the site of the wagon works. The picture is from 20th June 1964. (B.P.Mills)

117. The junction is seen on 27th March 1976 as the 18.27 Cardiff to Swansea approaches. By that time the line on the right ran only to the bay platform. Track remodelling took place in 1965 and was unchanged 40 years later. (T.Heavyside)

BRIDGEND

XLI. This map continues from the left of the previous one and shows the private sidings of R.S. & G.V.Hayes diverging from the bay loop. The siding from the up line on the right served Jenkin's limeworks. There were ten other private sidings listed in 1938. In 1930, there had been 99 men concerned with passenger operations and 26 on the goods side.

118.   Although undated, this westward panorama gives an excellent overview and includes the massive goods shed, which was in use until 19th July 1965. The up express is at platform 3. Barry trains used no. 1 on the left and trains to the valleys departed from no. 4. Its track was lifted later but was fully reinstated in 2005. (M.J.Stretton coll.)

119.   A photograph from May 1958 shows the earlier running-in board, which features the VoGR, a company that never operated a train itself. The Llynfi route lost its service in 1970 and Ogmore in 1958, but trains ran as far as Maesteg again from 1992 and a bay platform was created at the north end of the former No. 4. (G.Adams/M.J.Stretton coll.)

120.   No. 47509 hauled the 18.20 Swansea to Paddington on 27th March 1976 and three years later the station was modernised, but part of the down side building was retained, as it had been listed Grade II. The 1887 footbridge was also kept. The bay on the left would receive trains from Barry again in 2005, after an interval of 41 years, the mail traffic having long gone. (T.Heavyside)

MP **Middleton Press**

EVOLVING THE ULTIMATE RAIL ENCYCLOPEDIA

Easebourne Lane, Midhurst, West Sussex.
GU29 9AZ Tel:01730 813169

www.middletonpress.co.uk   email:info@middletonpress.co.uk
A-0 906520   B-1 873793   C-1 901706   D-1 904474

OOP Out of Print at time of printing - Please check current availability **BROCHURE AVAILABLE SHOWING NEW TITLES**